World Food Supply

This is a volume in the Arno Press collection

World Food Supply

Advisory Editor
D. Gale Johnson

Editorial Board
Charles M. Hardin
Kenneth H. Parsons

See last pages of this volume for a complete list of titles.

Jefferson and Agriculture

Compiled and Edited
by
EVERETT E. EDWARDS

ARNO PRESS
A New York Times Company
New York — 1976

Editorial Supervision: MARIE STARECK

Reprint Edition 1976 by Arno Press Inc.

Reprinted from a copy in
  The Princeton University Library

WORLD FOOD SUPPLY
ISBN for complete set: 0-405-07766-1
See last pages of this volume for titles.

Manufactured in the United States of America

Library of Congress Cataloging in Publication Data

Edwards, Everett Eugene, 1900-   comp.
    Jefferson and agriculture.

    (World food supply)
    Reprint of the 1943 ed. published by the Dept. of
Agriculture, Washington, which was issued as no. 7 of
Agricultural history series.
    "Selected references concerning Jefferson": p.
    1. Jefferson, Thomas, Pres. U. S., 1743-1826.
2. Agriculture--United States. I. Title. II. Series.
III. Series: United States. Bureau of Agricultural
Economics. Agricultural history series ; no. 7.
E332.2.E38   1976   630'.973   75-27636
ISBN 0-405-07778-5

Jefferson
and
Agriculture

A Sourcebook Compiled and Edited

by

EVERETT E. EDWARDS

BUREAU OF AGRICULTURAL ECONOMICS

United States Department of Agriculture
In Commemoration of the Two Hundredth Anniversary
of the Birth of Thomas Jefferson

1943

AGRICULTURAL HISTORY SERIES NO. 7

FOREWORD

The year 1943 marks the two hundredth anniversary of the birth of Thomas Jefferson. In this time of world struggle to retain the principles of freedom which he enunciated, it is fitting that we recall his public services as the writer of the Declaration of Independence, Governor of Virginia, Minister to France, Secretary of State, and as President of the United States. It is, however, equally important that we recognize his pioneering efforts in the field of agriculture. Eminently versatile and farsighted, he was among the first to become interested in many phases of the work now pursued by the United States Department of Agriculture and the Land-Grant Colleges for the general welfare. It is appropriate, therefore, that these two institutions, along with agricultural societies, farm organizations, and farmers themselves should join together in commemorating his bicentenary.

There are, of course, many ways in which the occasion might be marked, but an informing and satisfying way is to let Jefferson himself tell us of the importance of agriculture in the Nation's economy; of his own deep love of farming; of his never-ending search for improved methods, labor-saving implements and machines, and better crops and livestock; and of his views on agricultural education, experimentation, and cooperative action. The selections from Jefferson's writings here included have been arranged by Everett E. Edwards of the Bureau of Agricultural Economics with this purpose in mind.

Claude R. Wickard
Secretary of Agriculture

JEFFERSON AND AGRICULTURE: A SOURCEBOOK
COMPILED AND EDITED BY EVERETT E. EDWARDS

CONTENTS

	Page
Introductory Note	1
Chronology of Significant Events in the Life of Jefferson	3

PART I
JEFFERSON'S CONTRIBUTIONS

Thomas Jefferson; Farmer, Educator, and Democrat, by Henry A. Wallace, Vice President of the United States	5
Thomas Jefferson – Farmer, by M. L. Wilson, Director of Extension Work, United States Department of Agriculture	14

PART II
SELECTIONS FROM JEFFERSON'S WRITINGS

Jefferson's Views on the Nature of the National Economy

Farmers are God's Chosen People	23
Advantages of an Agricultural Economy	24
The Place of Commerce	25
Agriculture as the Source of Virtue, Freedom, and Happiness	25
The Dangers of Urbanization	26
The Frontier as a Safety-valve	26
The Place of Manufacturing	27
Equilibrium of Agriculture, Manufactures, and Commerce	28

Jefferson's Observations on Agriculture in Europe and the United States

English Agriculture	29
French Agriculture	29
Agriculture in Virginia	30
Differences between the Political Economy of Europe and America	31
Albemarle County, Virginia	32

Page

Jefferson's Farming Activities

    Jefferson's Love of Farming 35
    Jefferson's Farm Book 36
    Jefferson's Garden Book 38
    Implements and Machinery 39
    Rotations 45
    Erosion Control 46
    Crops 47
    Livestock 49
    Household Manufactures 51
    Sharing with Others 52

Jefferson and the Advancement of Agriculture

    Democratization of Land Holding 54
    Settlement of the Public Domain 55
    Indian Policy 56
    Trade Promotion 57
    Slavery 60
    Patents 61
    Plant Exploration and Introduction 66
    Experimentation 71
    Societies 72
    Libraries 78
    Education 81

Selected References Concerning Jefferson 85
Index 87

INTRODUCTORY NOTE

Jefferson's life was largely spent in the political service of the Nation which he did so much to help create and whose future course of development he did so much to chart. Often referred to as the apostle of democracy, his political principles have become interwoven with the consciousness of the American multitude. More clearly than any of his contemporaries he comprehended the forces that were moulding the American political and social structure. Consciously he assumed the leadership of these forces, and as a result the United States became a democracy. Furthermore, it has remained so largely because of his eminent leadership. Thus, his personality permeated that of his own country and ultimately extended its influence to many other lands.

Jefferson was born near the frontier of colonial Virginia, and the democracy he enunciated was in essence the product of the type of society that gave him life and nurtured him during his formative years. It was on the frontier that age-old traditions, class distinctions, and family prestige - the complexes that differentiated the traditional European civilization from the American - disintegrated and disappeared, and it was to their uprooting and destruction that Jefferson dedicated his life. The study and thinking of his mature years merely resulted in a rationalization of the heritage from his frontier past. The frontier was agricultural and therefore eminently practical. Likewise is Jefferson's philosophy practical, and its roots, like his, were embedded in an agricultural background.

Shortly before his death, Jefferson designated the Declaration of Independence, the Virginia Statute of Religious Freedom, and the founding of the University of Virginia as the chief contributions of his life. In retrospect it is apparent that Jefferson's judgment of his own services was as unerring as had been his vision of his country's life. The first had provided a creed for democracy. The second was a milestone in the age-long struggle to separate civil governments from religious domination or influence. In one succinct sentence, he disposed of the divergent contentions of centuries. "The opinions of men are not the object of civil government, nor under its jurisdiction." Thus, toleration for minority opinions, religious or otherwise, gained a final triumph. Third, but not least, Jefferson realized that if democracy was to survive it must be an intelligent democracy. He therefore did all within his power to further the cause of general education in America. His projected curriculum for education embraced all branches of human knowledge. The sovereignty of human reason was to be enthroned, and all things were to be subjected to investigation and skeptical analysis before acceptance.

In addition to leadership in the achievement of democracy, Jefferson made other notable contributions to the framework of the American empire. In the critical period following the recognition of American independence, the question of how the new Nation was to govern its public domain arose. Jefferson was chairman of the committee selected to draft a plan of government for this domain. His report was adopted, with changes, as the Ordinance of 1784. It embraced the general principle that the regions west of the Alleghenies were to have restricted rights of self-government during sparse settlement and were ultimately to be admitted to the Union on terms of equality with the

Thirteen Original States. Thus, the problem of empire which had shaken and ultimately broken the British Empire in the years immediately following 1763 was on its way toward solution. The Ordinance of 1784 was a forecast of future development.

Jefferson also served as chairman of the committee that outlined the general principles of American land policy in the Ordinance of 1785. The draft of the committee report in 1784 is in his handwriting, but he retired from the chairmanship and went to Europe to serve as minister to France before the Ordinance was adopted by Congress in 1785. The Ordinance embodied the fundamentals of the American land system which, with modifications dictated by experience, proved to be permanently workable.

It was Jefferson who grasped the significance of possible American acquisition of the vast territory to the west of the Mississippi River, then known in a general way as Louisiana, and initiated the steps that resulted in its purchase from Napoleon. As an immediate result the pioneers of Tennessee, Kentucky, and Ohio gained a free outlet for their products by way of the Mississippi to the sea. Most important was the acquisition of the vast imperial domain stretching from the great interior valley of America westward to the Pacific as a region where thousands of American farm homes could be developed in the future.

The interests of Jefferson were not limited to political leadership and statesmanship. His curiosity about men and things was omnivorous and insatiable, and his writings indicate that he was abreast of the latest developments in practically every field of knowledge. Possessed of the scientific spirit, he made contributions to the fields of geography, botany, paleontology, ethnology, and natural history, and his interest in mechanics resulted in his inventing numerous ingenious as well as practical appliances.

Jefferson was a practitioner as well as a patron of the arts. Perhaps most noteworthy in this field is his work as an architect. His design for the State House at Richmond set the architectural pattern for public buildings in America for over a century. His beloved Monticello and the famous quadrangle at the University of Virginia are likewise notable contributions to American architecture.

Reference has already been made to the agricultural antecedents of Jefferson's genius. As a farmer he sought to make Monticello and his other landholdings profitable as well as self-sufficient. This fact, together with his scientific inclinations, resulted in Monticello's becoming a progressive experimental farm where new machinery, new methods, and new crops were tried out. Over a long period he grew as many as thirty-two different vegetables at Monticello, and he attempted to adapt, domesticate, or acclimatize literally scores of plants, shrubs, and trees. In some cases he succeeded; in others, he failed.

Jefferson also applied his scientific knowledge and ability to the problems of improving farm machinery. In this field of activity, his chief contribution was a moldboard that turned the soil with the least possible resistance. He also developed other farm devices, including a seed drill, a hemp brake, and improvements on a threshing machine. No less than four hundred and fifty of the extant personal letters to friends and acquaintances deal primarily with agricultural matters, and these, together with his Farm Book and Garden Book afford ample testimony of his eminence as a statesman in the field of agriculture.

To Jefferson, agriculture was more than an occupation; it was a way of life. In his belief, it developed social virtues that were peculiar to tillers of the soil — virtues that were basic in the life of any great nation. Agriculture was the basis of his philosophy and the source of his strength.

The interpretations of Jefferson as a farmer and the excerpts from his writings that follow have been selected and arranged with a view to illustrating and emphasizing Jefferson's agricultural interests and contributions.

CHRONOLOGY OF SIGNIFICANT EVENTS IN THE LIFE OF JEFFERSON

1743 Apr. 13   Born at Shadwell, Albemarle County, Virginia, in the foothills of the Blue Ridge Mountains

1757 Aug. 17   Death of his father, Peter Jefferson

1760 Mar. 25   Entered the College of William and Mary at Williamsburg, Virginia

1762 Apr. 25   Graduated from the College of William and Mary and began the study of law in the office of George Wythe at Williamsburg

1767   Admitted to the bar of Virginia

1769   Elected a member of the House of Burgesses from Shadwell, serving in that body during its intermittent sessions from May 8, 1769 to June 11, 1775

1770 Nov. 26   Moved to Monticello

1772 Jan. 1   Married Martha Wayles Skelton

1774   Wrote his celebrated *Summary View of the Rights of British America*, protesting the recent actions of the British Government and foreshadowing the Declaration of Independence

1775   Became member of the Second Continental Congress at Philadelphia, serving from June 21, 1775 to Sept. 2, 1776

1776 July 4   Adoption of the Declaration of Independence as drafted by Jefferson

     Oct. 7   Assumed seat in the Virginia Legislature where he served until his election as Governor

1777   Served as member of a committee to revise the laws and constitution of Virginia

1779 June 1   Elected Governor of Virginia and served until his resignation on June 1, 1781

1781	July	Began preparation of his *Notes on Virginia*
1782	Sept. 6	Death of his wife, Martha Jefferson
1783	June 6	Elected to the Congress of the Confederation where he served until July 5, 1784
1784	May 23	His ordinance on western lands considered and adopted by the Congress
	July 5	Sailed from Boston for Europe to serve as Minister Plenipotentiary to negotiate treaties of commerce
1785	Mar. 10	Elected Minister to France, succeeding Benjamin Franklin; published his *Notes on Virginia* in Paris
1789	Oct.	Returned to the United States
1790	Mar. 22	Became Secretary of State in President Washington's Cabinet
1793	Dec. 31	Resigned as Secretary of State and returned to Monticello
1797	Mar. 4	Became Vice President of the United States
1801	Mar. 4	Inaugurated as President of the United States at Washington, D. C., the new seat of the national government
1803	Jan. 18	Sent secret message to Congress asking an appropriation for the Lewis and Clark Expedition
	May 2	Treaty for purchase of Louisiana Territory signed at Paris
1809	Mar. 4	Retired as President and returned to Monticello
1814	Sept. 21	Offered his library to Congress to replace the one lost when the Capitol was burned
1825	Mar. 6	University of Virginia opened after approximately fifty years of planning by Jefferson
1826	July 4	Died at Monticello, on the fiftieth anniversary of the adoption of the Declaration of Independence

PART I

JEFFERSON'S CONTRIBUTIONS

THOMAS JEFFERSON; FARMER, EDUCATOR, AND DEMOCRAT

By

HENRY A. WALLACE
Vice President of the United States

This is no ordinary occasion. Nothing like this has ever happened before. The farmers of the United States through the Land-Grant Colleges and the Department of Agriculture have made this pilgrimage to Monticello to do reverence to a man who created in considerable measure the foundations on which they now stand.[1]

It was Jefferson more than any man of his time who foresaw the fruitfulness of the application of science to agriculture. It was Jefferson more than any man of his time who saw the need of a democratized education. It was Jefferson who was the very heart and soul of that democracy, that American ideal which all of us have held so dear.

But as we come to Jefferson today, we do so in the spirit not merely of reverencing what he did in the past but in the spirit which he would have applied to the future.

Yes, we are met here today at Monticello to do honor to a great farmer, a great educator, and a great democrat. From the standpoint of ideas and philosophy, he was the most cultured American of his day and perhaps of our entire history. From a philosophic point of view, he was perhaps as much the father of his country as George Washington. But because he was a man of ideas and expressed them freely, we find in his life many apparent contradictions which can be reconciled only as we become acquainted with the full man.

To get acquainted with Jefferson and the living Monticello of Jefferson's day, I am going to ask you to travel back with me to the time when Jefferson had retired from the Presidency and the Napoleonic Wars were in full swing. He was sixty-nine years old here on this very hilltop at Monticello when a letter was brought to him which had taken twenty-one days in traveling from Quincy, Massachusetts. It was from John Adams, who for many years had been his bitter enemy. They had run against each

---

[1] On November 14-17, 1937, the Association of Land-Grant Colleges and Universities and the United States Department of Agriculture held a joint program to commemorate the seventy-fifth anniversary of the establishment of the land-grant colleges and the United States Department of Agriculture and the fiftieth anniversary of the Hatch Act which provided Federal aid for the experiment stations. On the third day, the delegates and visitors journeyed to Charlottesville, Virginia, where they made a tour of the campus of the University of Virginia. At noon, they assembled in the University Auditorium where the Secretary of Agriculture, Henry A. Wallace, presented the notable address which is here printed with his permission. It was originally published in the Association of Land-Grant Colleges and Universities, *Proceedings*, 51:338-346 (1937).

other for the Presidency in 1796 and Adams had won. From 1796 to 1800, these two co-signers of the Declaration of Independence gradually became as much opposed to each other as were Taft and Theodore Roosevelt in 1912. In 1800, Jefferson beat Adams. But after twelve years of separation, Adams suddenly broke the ice with a rather formal letter saying he was sending Jefferson a couple of pieces of homespun produced in his section of the country. Jefferson, not waiting for the homespun to arrive, was so touched by Adams' letter that he immediately sat down to write and took "homespun" for his text.[2] It was a subject in which he was greatly interested because his embargo laws, while he was President, had proved perhaps to be a greater stimulus to manufacturing than any tariff conceived by Alexander Hamilton. This letter of Jefferson written to Adams in 1812 is of an especial interest because it gives us an idea of the kind of living which went on here at Monticello at that time. Jefferson, after admitting the superiority of New England homespuns, wrote:

Here we do little in the fine way, but in coarse and middling goods a great deal. Every family in the country is a manufactory within itself, and is very generally able to make within itself all the stouter and middling stuffs for its own clothing and household use. We consider a sheep for every person in the family as sufficient to clothe it, in addition to the cotton, hemp and flax which we raise ourselves. For fine stuff we shall depend on your northern manufactories. Of these, that is to say, of company establishments, we have none. We use little machinery. The spinning jenny, and loom with the flying shuttle, can be managed in a family; but nothing more complicated. The economy and thriftiness resulting from our household manufactures are such that they will never again be laid aside; and nothing more salutary for us has ever happened than the British obstructions to our demands for their manufactures. Restore free intercourse when they will, their commerce with us will have totally changed its form, and the articles we shall in future want from them will not exceed their own consumption of our produce.[3]

Following this the old man became sentimental about how he and Adams had pulled together back in 1776 and how now all but seven of the signers of the Declaration were dead.

With this interchange between the friendly old enemies in 1812, there began a correspondence which continued until death fourteen years later. They exchanged over two hundred letters. The two old boys warmed up to each other and wrote their hearts out, probing the meaning of religion, aristocracy, grief, and science. One of Jefferson's last letters, written in 1825 when he was past eighty, describes the experiments of a Frenchman who compared the reactions of animals which had their cerebrums removed with other animals which had their cerebellums removed. That a man of eighty should deal so accurately with an analytical scientific subject is rather remarkable. Adams, who was past ninety, came back with the statement:

Incision-knives will never discover the distinction between matter and spirit, or whether there is any or not. That there is an active principle of power in the universe, is apparent; but in what substance that principle resides, is past our investigation. The faculties of our understanding are not adequate to penetrate the universe.[4]

---

[2]Jefferson took Adams literally, but Adams hastened to explain that "The Material of the Samples of American Manufacture which I sent you, was not Wool, nor Cotton, nor Silk nor Flax nor Hemp nor Iron nor Wood. They were spun from the brain of John Quincy Adams and consist in two Volumes of his Lectures on Rhetorick and oratory, delivered when he was Prof ssor of that Science in our University of Cambridge." Adams to Jefferson, Feb. 3, 1812, in Paul Wilstach, ed., *Correspondence of John Adams and Thomas Jefferson* (Indianapolis, 1925).

[3]Jefferson to John Adams, from Monticello, Jan. 21, 1812. See p. 51-52 for the entire letter.

[4]John Adams to Jefferson, from Quincy, Mass., Jan. 22, 1825, in John Adams, *Works, with a Life of the Author, Notes, and Illustrations*, edited by Charles Francis Adams, 10:414 (Boston, 1856).

When these two old men died at the same hour on July 4, 1826, two of the most remarkable men of American history passed on.

Six days before Adams decided to open correspondence with Jefferson, he wrote to a friend very critically about Jefferson's administration, taking him to task especially for his failure to build a navy and for his embargo act. Adams said:

We differed in opinion about the French revolution. He thought it wise and good, and that it would end in the establishment of a free republic. I saw through it, to the end of it, before it broke out, and was sure it could end only in a restoration of the Bourbons, or a military despotism, after deluging France and Europe in blood.[5]

He went on to express the view that Jefferson may have been swayed a little too much by ambition and love of popularity. And yet after voicing various criticisms, he stated that Jefferson was not his enemy but his friend. Six days later, he proved it by opening up the correspondence which came to mean so much to both.

In this indirect manner, I hope I have today warmed your minds a little bit to Jefferson as a human being and as distinct from that man on the pedestal who wrote the Declaration of Independence. First and foremost Jefferson was a farmer. He loved the land and the people who lived on it. It is hard to say whether he loved the farmers because he thought them essential to democracy or whether he loved democracy because it gave full expression to farmers. The two went hand-in-hand in Jefferson's mind, and his faith in farmers and democracy as a keystone of government explains nearly all the apparent contradictions of his political life. He hated and feared cities. Within a few months after the Constitution was drafted, he wrote Madison from Paris to say that "our governments will remain virtuous for many centuries; as long as they are chiefly agricultural; and this will be as long as there shall be vacant lands in any part of America. When they get piled upon one another in large cities, as in Europe, they will become corrupt as in Europe."[6]

Perhaps because of inborn love of the soil, perhaps because of the relationship between farmers and democracy, Jefferson undertook to live on the soil and to build a community according to his heart's desire here at Monticello. What a hive of industry was this hilltop in those days! Monticello sold very little to the outside world and bought very little from it. Not only did it produce its own food but also its own clothing, lumber, fuel, nails, and bricks. Over these workmen and farmers, Jefferson presided as the architect and planner. While apparently he got a great joy out of building and inventing various contrivances, he evidently got his greatest pleasure out of agricultural experimenting. He tried to prevent soil erosion by plowing around the slope instead of up and down the slope. He applied the science of physics to the problem of working out the kind of a moldboard to a plow which would meet the least resistance. He invented a seed drill and experimented with various types of rotations. That a private individual with such slender resources should be able to do such sound pioneering in agricultural experimental work, along with his other activities, is one of the miracles of American history. He was not only interested in improving agricultural methods on his own land but also in spreading the knowledge to other farmers. To this end, he helped set up agricultural societies. It will interest you who are here

---

[5] John Adams to Benjamin Rush, from Quincy, Mass., Dec. 25, 1811, in *ibid.*, 10:11.
[6] Jefferson to James Madison, from Paris, Dec. 20, 1787. See p. 26.

assembled representing the Land-Grant Colleges of the United States and who have to do with the most powerful agricultural educational movement in the entire world to know that Thomas Jefferson did his best to get a professor of agriculture included in the faculty of the University of Virginia.

When we turn to Jefferson, the educator, we find that his belief in education, like his belief in agriculture, was largely related to his faith in democracy as the best type of government. He knew that democracy could not work unless there was popular education among the people. Jefferson fought for universal elementary education at public expense at a time when the "Jeffersonian Democrats" of that day were horrified at the thought of such a radical measure. Jefferson, as a farmer, believed that farmers were just as good as anybody else if they had a chance to get educated, and he proposed to see that they had the chance. Educated farmers were the stuff out of which democracy could be built. To that faith Jefferson gave most of his life.

By education Jefferson meant something more than mere literacy. To him a public school system in which the rudiments were taught was necessary to the Nation's future. But, in addition, he believed in higher education, as his founding of the University of Virginia shows. And if his own life is any indication, he did not hold that the educational process came to a close with the end of one's formal schooling. Instead, to him all life was education. As one who appreciated the scientific method, Jefferson respected objective facts. As a believer in democracy he displayed his faith in the capacities of common men to govern themselves in the light of the facts around them.

Many people make much out of the contradiction between Jefferson, the States' righter, and Jefferson, the President. It is true that when Jefferson was out of power and was fighting men in power who represented, according to his ideas, the city aristocracy, he fought for States' rights. It is also true that when he himself got into power he used the Federal power in a very broad way, first to buy the Louisiana Territory, and, second, to embargo foreign trade. He hated the Supreme Court with a greater hate than any President before or since, and there have been many good haters. Jefferson, with his agricultural Virginia background, no doubt thought that his activities as President were fundamentally sound. But New England, with her industrial trading and banking activities, was terribly angered by them.

The Embargo Act was probably the most sweeping use of power ever employed by the Federal Government in time of peace. New England at the time of the Louisiana Purchase feared the day when a flock of Western States would enter the Union with more farmers and thus dilute the seaboard influence. One hundred years before Senator George H. Moses, the fear of the "Sons of the Wild Jackass" was to be found in New England. New England and the Middle States were therefore sure that the Louisiana Purchase was unconstitutional. They felt the same way about the embargo acts which interfered so grievously with New England shipping. William Cullen Bryant, one of the best loved of American poets, put the feelings of New England into verse:

> Go, wretch, resign the presidential chair,
> Disclose thy secret measures, foul or fair.
> Go, search with curious eye, for horned frogs,
> Mid the wild wastes of Louisianian bogs.[7]

---

[7] William Cullen Bryant, *The Embargo; or, Sketches of the Times* (ed. 2, Boston, 1809).

For thwarting the will of the rich and the well-born and throwing his lot with the small farmers, Jefferson drew upon himself much more violent abuse than the doggerel of Bryant. Most of the well-to-do people called him a "Jacobin" with the same feeling of righteous abhorrence well-to-do people speak today of communists. Many ministers hated him because he had been active in disestablishing the church in Virginia and therefore he was often called an atheist or an anarchist. In this connection for the purpose of keeping the record straight it is worth quoting the following from Claude G. Bowers:

While the New England pulpits were ringing with denunciations of this 'infidel,' and old ladies, unable to detect the false witness of the partisan clergy, were solemnly hiding their Bibles to prevent their confiscation by the 'atheist' in the President's House, he was spending his nights in the codification of the 'Morals of Jesus,' and through the remainder of his life he was to read from this every night before retiring. In his last days he spent much time reading the Greek dramatists and the Bible, dwelling in conversation on the superiority of the moral system of Christ over all others. In his dying hour, after taking leave of his family, he was heard to murmur, 'Lord, now lettest Thy servant depart in peace.'[8]

Hamilton claimed that only the rich and the well-born were fit to govern and that the people could not be trusted to judge aright. The followers of Hamilton attacked Jefferson as a leader of "desperate, embarrassed, unprincipled, disorderly, ambitious, disaffected, morose men." They were said to be popular only in "barrooms" and "alehouses."[9] The leading Federalist newspaper called Jefferson an "assassin" and a "liar."[10] The rich and the well-born ostracized Jefferson socially so that in 1797 he wrote to Edward Rutledge that "Men who have been intimate all their lives, cross the streets to avoid meeting, and turn their heads another way, lest they should be obliged to touch their hats."[11]

Of course, the irresponsible elements in both parties engaged in their usual underhanded mud-slinging practices, but probably no man in American history has been the object of so many wild accusations by the rich and the well-born. For example, the Chief Justice of Massachusetts in 1798 denounced Jefferson and his followers as "apostles of atheism and anarchy, bloodshed and plunder." The brother of the president of Yale College in 1801, shortly after Jefferson took office as President, made an oration in which he contended that, "We have a country governed by blockheads and knaves," and "Jacobinism will now destroy civilization."[12] A Justice of the Supreme Court of the United States, denouncing the Jeffersonians, said, "The modern doctrines of our late reformers that all men in a state of society are entitled to enjoy equal liberty and equal rights have brought this mighty mischief upon us. I fear it will rapidly progress until peace and order, freedom and property, shall be destroyed."[13] One of the first moves of the Jeffersonians when coming into power was to unpack the Federal courts which had been packed by Adams with aristocratic Federalists just before Jefferson came into power. As a result of the unpacking effort Jefferson was accused

---

[8] Claude G. Bowers, *Jefferson and Hamilton: The Struggle for Democracy in America*, 103 (Boston and New York, 1925).

[9] *Ibid.*, 152.

[10] *Ibid.*, 352.

[11] Jefferson to Edward Rutledge, from Philadelphia, June 24, 1797, in H. A. Washington, ed., *The Writings of Thomas Jefferson*, 4:191 (Washington, D. C., 1854). Hereafter, this work is referred to as the Washington ed.

[12] Quoted in Claude G. Bowers, *Jefferson in Power*, 71 (Boston, 1936).

[13] Quoted in *ibid.*, 274.

in the most violent terms of wanting to destroy the Federal judiciary and subject all things to his will. During the debate in Congress over the embargo, a New York Federalist declared that Jefferson took his orders from Napoleon. In New York State in 1808, the Fourth of July was celebrated by the Federalists hanging the President of the United States and the author of the Declaration of Independence in effigy.

Jefferson lived through the attacks of the rich and well-born opponents and maintained a sweet spirit. When he was seventy-three years old, he wrote John Adams:

You ask, if I would agree to live my seventy or rather seventy-three years over again? To which I say, yea. I think with you, that it is a good world on the whole; that it has been framed on a principle of benevolence, and more pleasure than pain dealt out to us. . . . My temperament is sanguine. I steer my bark with Hope in the head, leaving Fear astern. My hopes, indeed, sometimes fail; but not oftener than the forebodings of the gloomy.[14]

We can only guess what Jefferson would say and do today. He would be puzzled to find present in the United States the great cities which he so hated in Europe. His first thought would be to tremble for the Nation because of the fact that there was no more free land and, therefore, people would begin to pile upon one another and to eat one another. He would not at first understand the great corporations and the labor unions in the large cities. His first instinct perhaps might be to break up the large cities and to destroy the corporations. We know that he hated monopolies and wrote from Paris at the time of the Constitution trying to get an amendment included in the Bill of Rights prohibiting monopolies. We know, furthermore, that Massachusetts and New Hampshire voted also to have the antimonopoly amendment included in the Bill of Rights.

Jefferson, the man who wanted an amendment to the Constitution prohibiting monopoly, would be aghast at our billion-dollar corporations. Jefferson, who abolished primogeniture and entail in Virginia in order to prevent monopoly in land, would be appalled by our high percentage of tenancy. Jefferson, as the man who dreaded the day when many of our citizens might become landless, would perhaps feel our civilization was trembling on the brink of ruin, if he were to find so many of our people without either land or tools, and subject to the hire and power of distant corporations. If the Jefferson of 1820 could see his name used by men crying "States' rights!" in order to protect not individual liberties but corporate property, then he *would* shudder.

But Jefferson, of all men, expected change. He believed that human institutions should be adjusted to the facts of a changing world. His first glimpse of the present social and economic organization of the United States would no doubt cause surprise, horror, and indignation, but a second and longer look would reconcile him to the necessity of living with corporations, labor unions, and other pressure groups, and of making them serve the General Welfare.

Jefferson was an inventor, especially of agricultural machinery, but he would be astounded beyond measure to observe that today there is only one farm family to three town and city families in the United States whereas in his day there were nine farm families to one family living in town and city. He would be fascinated by the inventions which released so many farm people to go to town but would be gravely disturbed about the economic, sociological, and political consequences.

---

[14]Jefferson to John Adams, from Monticello, Apr. 8, 1816, in Washington ed., 6:575.

Somehow I am inclined to think that if Jefferson were to come back today he would adapt himself to the changed situation with remarkable skill, but hold fast to one thing above everything else – his belief in democracy. Even his belief in the need for the majority of our people being farmers might fade under the impact of events. His adaptability is illustrated by his change in attitude with regard to manufactures. When he was fighting Hamilton, he hated manufacturing because he thought it reduced the importance of agriculture and therefore the safety of democracy. But when he became president and England was preying upon our commerce he became converted to the need for a tariff to protect infant industries, defending his change in front when writing to an old friend by saying: "barefaced attempts [of England] to make us accessories and tributaries to her usurpations on the high seas, have generated in this country an universal spirit for manufacturing for ourselves, and of reducing to a minimum the number of articles for which we are dependent on her."[15]

Yes, Jefferson was a philosophical theorist but he could also be a practical man, and after he had lived out his two terms as president he expressed one of his wisest observations when he said:

An equilibrium of agriculture, manufactures, and commerce, is certainly become essential to our independence. Manufactures, sufficient for our own consumption, of what we raise the raw material (and no more). Commerce sufficient to carry the surplus produce of agriculture, beyond our own consumption, to a market for exchanging it for articles we cannot raise (and no more). These are the true limits of manufactures and commerce. To go beyond them is to increase our dependence on foreign nations, and our liability to war.[16]

Here we find clearly expressed for the first time as a fundamental principle of statesmanship that objective of balance which we are seeking today.

Jefferson could go with the times. He knew that he had changed when in 1816 he wrote, "You tell me I am quoted by those who wish to continue our dependence on England for manufactures. There was a time when I might have been so quoted with more candor, but within the thirty years which have since elapsed, how are circumstances changed! . . . experience has taught me that manufactures are now as necessary to our independence as to our comfort. . . ."[17]

However much Jefferson may have changed with respect to his attitude toward manufacturing and agriculture he never changed with respect to his views on democracy. He was for an educated democracy first, last, and all the time. He wanted it based preferably on farmers owning their own land. It was because of that that he did so much in an early day to abolish primogeniture and entail in Virginia. More than anyone else he was responsible for keeping English landlords out of the United States. More than anyone else he kept English aristocracy out of the United States, when the Federalists and especially Hamilton and Adams would have liked to introduce it. In all of this he never changed. His attitude on States' rights might change but not his attitude on democracy. His fundamental thesis was to enable as many people as possible to own property, saying:

---

[15] Jefferson to Pierre Samuel Du Pont de Nemours, from Monticello, June 28, 1809, in Washington ed., 5:456.
[16] Jefferson to John Jay, from Monticello, Apr. 7, 1809. See p. 28, 57.
[17] Jefferson to Benjamin Austin, from Monticello, Jan. 9, 1816. See p. 27-28.

The earth is given as a common stock for man to labor and live on. If for the encouragement of industry we allow it to be appropriated, we must take care that other employment be provided for those excluded from the appropriation. If we do not, the fundamental right to labor the earth returns to the unemployed. It is too soon yet in our country to say that every man who cannot find employment, but who can find uncultivated land, shall be at liberty to cultivate it, paying a moderate rent. But it is not too soon to provide by every possible means that as few as possible shall be without a little portion of land. The small landholders are the most precious part of a state.[18]

Because of the tendency of debts periodically to crush small men he took a leaf out of the Bible and advocated that debts should be cancelled. But instead of advocating that this be done every seven years or every forty-nine years he suggested twenty years as most appropriate.

Of all the men of his day he most realized the probability of change and thought that written constitutions should be completely revised every twenty years. He feared that otherwise one generation might prey upon the generation succeeding it. When he was seventy-three years old his views on this subject were as follows:

But I know also, that laws and institutions must go hand in hand with the progress of the human mind. As that becomes more developed, more enlightened, as new discoveries are made, new truths disclosed, and manners and opinions change with the change of circumstances, institutions must advance also, and keep pace with the times. We might as well require a man to wear still the coat which fitted him when a boy, as civilized society to remain ever under the regimen of their barbarous ancestors. It is this preposterous idea which has lately deluged Europe in blood. Their monarchs, instead of wisely yielding to the gradual change of circumstances, of favoring progressive accommodation to progressive improvement, have clung to old abuses, entrenched themselves behind steady habits, and obliged their subjects to seek through blood and violence rash and ruinous innovations, which, had they been referred to the peaceful deliberations and collected wisdom of the nation, would have been put into acceptable and salutary forms. Let us follow no such examples, nor weakly believe that one generation is not as capable as another of taking care of itself, and of ordering its own affairs.

Jefferson's views on this subject were so forthright and he had suffered so much earlier in his life from the public press that he closed this particular letter with the following:

These, Sir, are my opinions of the governments we see among men, and of the principles by which alone we may prevent our own from falling into the same dreadful track. I have given them at greater length than your letter called for. But I cannot say things by halves; and I confide them to your honor, so to use them as to preserve me from the gridiron of the public papers.[19]

It should be said, however, that while Jefferson had suffered from the gridiron of the press he had the highest esteem for it as a mechanism of democracy and wrote on one occasion: " . . . were it left to me to decide whether we should have a government without newspapers, or newspapers without a government, I should not hesitate a moment to prefer the latter."[20]

It is worth while speculating on Jefferson's attitude toward the celebrated due-process clauses of the Fifth and Fourteenth amendments, which taken together guarantee that neither the Federal nor the State governments shall deprive any person of life, liberty, or property without due process of law. When Jefferson wrote the Declaration of Independence he used the phrase "life, liberty, and the pursuit of

---

[18] Jefferson to the Rev. James Madison, from Fontainbleau, Oct. 28, 1785, in Andrew A. Lipscomb and Albert Ellery Bergh, eds., *The Writings of Thomas Jefferson*, 19:18 (Washington, D. C., 1903).

[19] Jefferson to Samuel Kercheval, from Monticello, July 12, 1816, in Washington ed., 7:15, 17.

[20] Jefferson to Edward Carrington, from Paris, Jan. 16, 1787, in Washington ed., 2:100.

happiness," instead of "life, liberty, and property," which was the phrase which had come down out of the past in England. Again, when he was in Paris and was called upon to make suggestions with regard to the French declaration of the rights of man, he advised striking out "the right of property." He said it was not one of the natural rights. Jefferson was so much concerned that small farmers should have property and so fearful of the abuse of property rights that it is certain he would be enormously interested in the way the courts have applied the Fifth and Fourteenth amendments to protect the property and power of great corporations. His first instinct undoubtedly would be to fight the corporations to a standstill, and to bring about a revision of the interpretation of the Fifth and Fourteenth amendments so that the word "person" would mean "person" and not corporation. However I am inclined, as I contemplate the extraordinary adaptability of Jefferson, to reach the conclusion that on second thought he would find great corporations so necessary to the present standard of living in the United States that he would be concerned in working out a philosophy for democratizing corporations. Jefferson was a practical man, and he believed in democracy. He believed that government was meant to be of service to all the people and not merely to the rich and the well-born. He was in favor of the type of government which would promote the welfare of the greatest number of people. If under certain circumstances States' rights would do that, he wanted States' rights. If under other circumstances the exercise of Federal power would do it, he wanted Federal power. He won his great battle with Hamilton, and America became a democratic republic, not an oligarchy nor a monarchy. He lost his long battle with John Marshall, and the Supreme Court assumed the power he believed should reside in the people.

Jefferson adopted various expedients to meet the various problems of his own day. He always met those problems with the faith that government should be democratic and that government should adopt whatever measures are necessary to carry out the demands and meet the needs of the majority of the people.

I believe those principles still endure, and I believe shall long endure. They comprise the lesson that Jefferson has for us today, the lesson of government controlled by the people and in the interest of the people and government with the power to effect the program demanded by the people. It is a lesson that can hardly be repeated too often. Some people have recently repeated a slogan, "Back to Jefferson." I should like to amend it. We must go *forward* to Jefferson.

THOMAS JEFFERSON — FARMER

By

M. L. WILSON
*Director of Extension Work
United States Department of Agriculture*

Whatever Jefferson did he did with his whole heart and being.[1] Endowed with strong mental health, he found life never dull, never boresome; for him, it was filled with the wonders of nature, the growing things of the earth. While Minister to France he longed for Monticello. As his period as Secretary of State drew to a close, he wrote, "I am then to be liberated from the hated occupations of politics and to remain in the bosom of my family, my farm, and my books."[2] In 1794, after eighteen years of public service, counting from his election as delegate to the Continental Congress through his tenure as Secretary of State, he wrote: "I return to farming with an ardor which I scarcely knew in my youth."[3] Back at Monticello after his presidency, he stated, "No occupation is so delightful to me as the culture of the earth. . . ."[4]

We think of Jefferson as a great statesman, but more than this he was a statesman who lived on the land and liked farming. He was a good farmer, but as such we might never have heard of him. Many good farmers have made real contributions to agriculture, but, despite their part in the advance of husbandry, so close were they to the land, so far beyond the purview of historians, that their names all too frequently are unmarked in standard histories. Indeed, as to Jefferson himself, though all his biographers mention his farming, some giving a chapter, others a few paragraphs, many have missed the significance of his work. He was the scientist in the field. Agriculture, he believed, "is a science of the very first order. It counts among its handmaids the most respectable sciences, such as Chemistry, Natural Philosophy, Mechanics, Mathematics generally, Natural History, Botany."[5]

IMPORTANCE OF AGRICULTURAL HISTORY

Jefferson's first great biographer, Henry Stephens Randall, practical farmer and noted writer on farming practices, was keenly appreciative of Jefferson's part in the development of American agriculture. But the full-length life history which he undertook, with a devoted political partisanship, was of such scope that the space given farming was necessarily limited. Today, however, the Agricultural History

---

[1]This address was presented before the American Philosophical Society at Philadelphia on Apr. 22, 1943. It is here printed from the American Philosophical Society, *Proceedings*, 87:216-222 (1943), with the permission of the author and the Society.

[2]Jefferson to Mrs. Angelica Church, from Germantown, Pa., Nov. 27, 1793. See p. 35 for the letter.

[3]Jefferson to John Adams, from Monticello, Apr. 25, 1794. See p. 35.

[4]Jefferson to Charles Willson Peale, from Poplar Forest, Aug. 20, 1811. See p. 36.

[5]Jefferson to David Williams, from Washington, D. C., Nov. 14, 1803. See p. 81-82.

Society, now in its twenty-fourth year, is emphasizing importance of historical interpretation from the agricultural, as well as the primary social, political, and economic viewpoints. If we are to know our present culture, we must understand our agricultural past.

Here, in this paper, some use has been made of but a small portion of the great body of agricultural materials which center about Jefferson's name. Only a portion of his total correspondence has been published; and in that portion, editors, working from a particular viewpoint, have sometimes made regrettable omissions of agricultural material. Were the whole body of materials related to his farming available today, we would know more about Thomas Jefferson, the farmer, and also more about the great advance of agriculture in which he participated.

LEADERS IN AGRICULTURE

Born in 1743 in the farmhouse, Shadwell, located on the heavy red Davidson soils of Albemarle County, Virginia, Jefferson was a prophet and a leader in the development of scientific agriculture in America. As a world figure in the profession, he was internationally known and honored by agricultural societies in Great Britain, France, and Italy as well as in our own country. In connection with the development of the arts and sciences, it is customary to hang pictures of significant figures in college and university classrooms and public halls. Archimedes may be seen in the mathematics classrooms, Herodotus in those of history, Faraday in the physics buildings, and Lavoisier in the chemistry halls. In the classrooms of the colleges of agriculture, in the vocational agricultural high schools, in the Grange halls, and the many meeting places of farmers today, the pictures of Washington and Jefferson nearly always hang side by side. Farmers are proud that the father of their country was a farmer, a good farm manager, and a practical farm businessman. But Jefferson's picture hangs among the immortals of agriculture for a different reason. As Vice President Henry A. Wallace has said, "It was Jefferson more than any man of his time who foresaw the fruitfulness of the application of science to agriculture."[8] We think of his greatness as a champion of the rights and as an example of the responsibilities of the individual. From the standpoint of agriculture, farmers identify him with the application of science to agriculture, the improvement of the plow, the advocacy of soil conservation, the development of the concept of the agricultural college, and the recognition of agriculture as a learned profession.

THE AGRICULTURAL REVOLUTION

Agriculture during Jefferson's lifetime was in a stage of transition. Science was still in its infancy, but the fetters of medievalism had been thrown off. Systematization of knowledge was taking place, and the enlightenment was spreading. The agricultural revolution to which pioneers such as Jethro Tull with his seed drills and intensive cultivation, Lord Townshend with rotations, and Robert Bakewell in cattle breeding, contributed so much, was in progress. The books of publicists, such as Arthur Young, were in wide circulation. Just as the work of James Watt, and of others who contributed to the industrial revolution, was a projection of the work of physical

---

[6]Henry A. Wallace, "Thomas Jefferson: Farmer, Educator, and Democrat." See p. 5.

scientists, so, supporting the technicians of agriculture, were the botanist Linnaeus, the chemist Lavoisier, and the many scientists who have contributed to our knowledge of the soil and growing things.

DEVELOPMENTS IN THE UNITED STATES

Leaders in the United States paid close attention to developments in the agricultural field. The minutes of the early agricultural society, the Philadelphia Society for the Promotion of Agriculture, record again and again not only appreciation of European innovations but original improvements as well as adaptations of European practices to American conditions. Washington, at Mount Vernon, interested in practical results, put many experiments into effect. Jefferson, at Monticello, had not only the care of a large estate but a fundamental training of such type and a pen of such facility as to enable him to contribute to the basic knowledge which served to carry the agricultural revolution forward.

Jefferson's early education was obtained in schools, located at some distance from the farmhouse, Shadwell, but his vacations were regularly spent at the home farm. At the College of William and Mary, he was fortunate in having as his teacher the natural philosopher, William Small, who had a deep effect on his character and who undoubtedly contributed much to his scientific turn of mind. After his admittance to the bar in 1767, Jefferson took charge of the family farms about Monticello and Shadwell. Available figures give some measure of his practical success in this respect. His inheritance of 1,900 acres was more than doubled before his marriage at the age of twenty-nine. The farms, all paid for, yielded an income of some $2,000 a year. In a land of corn and tobacco he preached and practiced diversified farming. Albemarle County, today, in present season is white with the apple blossom and pink with the bloom of the peach.

ACTIVITIES AT MONTICELLO

Jefferson's power of accurate observation with regard to plants, climate, and many other interests appear in his Garden Book. There is something symbolic of the growth of the Great West, the farming center of the world, in Jefferson's planting of corn and other seeds brought back by the Lewis and Clark Expedition. His background of learning is indicated by use of Linnaean as well as common terms. His Garden Book is a depository of aesthetic appreciation, literary allusion, and practical provision for the table. Quantitative expression illustrates his scientific bent. When the first strawberries were gathered, they were not just strawberries of about a certain size, but rather, as he wrote on April 28, 1767, exactly so many of them filled a cup. The use of hypothesis is frequent — if a workman can lay so much stone in a day, so much will be accomplished in a given period. In this book, as in his Farm Book, there are examples of the application of principles. The Farm Book is primarily topical in form. Under the section, "Aphorisms, Observations, Facts in Husbandry," are seventeen divisions dealing with various phases of farm operations and domestic manufactures which include milling, brewing, and nail and textile manufacture. Monticello was much more than a center of farming as we know it today. It was a small world, in a material way, practically sufficient unto itself.

AGRICULTURAL PHILOSOPHY

Grasping the very stuff of which farming is made, as a scientist in the field and a thinker with world vision, Jefferson visited, swapped seeds and tools, and talked operations with friends and neighbors. Correspondence with his brother Randolph, a dirt farmer down on the James River, deals in a homely affectionate way with gardening operations, sheep dogs, and many other farm matters. Jefferson, foe of primogeniture and entail, was a firm believer in the character and democratic qualities of the small farmer. His distrusted undue emphasis on industrialism as a disease which might destroy democracy, but this did not mean a lack of appreciation of its importance. He believed in an "equilibrium of agriculture, manufactures, and commerce."[7] In 1816, he stated, "Manufactures are now as necessary to our independence as to our comfort."[8]

THE AGRICULTURAL LIBRARY

The library has been one of the important elements in the development of scientific agriculture, and today we have great specialized agricultural libraries in the colleges of agriculture, the experiment stations, and the Department of Agriculture at Washington. But the great specialized library of Jefferson's time was at Monticello. Other libraries may have included more works in English, but Jefferson's collection included Latin, Greek, French, and Italian contributions as well as the standard English works such as those of Young. Side by side in the several classifications are the attendant sciences: chemistry, botany, zoology, mathematics, physics, and others. The monographs of Parmentier on the potato, Lasteyrie on sheep raising, and La Brousse on fig culture are listed. There are selections on entomology, beekeeping, and soil chemistry. The work of Robert Livingston on sheep and John Taylor of Caroline's *Arator* were on the shelves. Transactions and reports of agricultural and learned societies, including the American Philosophical Society, are included. In the botany section is a full set of the works of Linnaeus. Jefferson's work in the promotion of agricultural libraries was carried forward in 1820 when a selected reference list on agriculture, prepared by him, was published in the *American Farmer*.

THE WORLD PLANT MIGRATION

Jefferson gained stimulation from the intellectuals whom he met in Europe, but from the agricultural standpoint, the opportunity which his stay gave him to play a part in the great world plant migration is perhaps more important. In this he was one of the many figures from Aristotle to David Fairchild who have served mankind by distributing the fruits of the earth. As an agricultural representative of an agricultural country he was constantly on the lookout for new ideas. In 1787, he wrote: "I am never satiated with rambling through the fields and farms, examining the culture and cultivators, with a degree of curiosity which makes some take me to be a fool, and others to be much wiser than I am."[9] He sent seeds, cuttings, and observations on vineyards, the cultivation of fruits, the production of silk, the milling of rice, and

---

[7] Jefferson to John Jay, from Monticello, Apr. 7, 1809. See p. 28,57.
[8] Jefferson to Benjamin Austin, from Monticello, Jan. 9, 1816. See p. 27-28.
[9] Jefferson to Lafayette, from Nice, Apr. 11, 1787. See p. 29-30.

the manufacture of flour to his friends at home. In later years, he regarded his efforts on behalf of the cultivation of dry rice and the olive to have been particularly worthy of note. His correspondence with the South Carolina Society for Promoting and Improving Agriculture stresses the importance of experimentation in the development of husbandry. If, in a multitude of experiments, he stated, "we make one useful acquisition, it repays our trouble."[10] Such work, at present carried on in the United States Department of Agriculture's Division of Plant Exploration and Introduction, has in the last fifty years contributed much to the development of such economic crops as soybeans, durum wheat, lespedeza, and oranges, and many cold-, drought-, and disease-resistant fruits and crops.

AGRICULTURAL RESEARCH AND EXPERIMENTATION

Jefferson's stimulation to agricultural research among members of the American Philosophical Society appears in the minutes of the Society. Sometimes the meetings in the early days appear to have been rather small. On April 15, 1791, with ten members present, his motion for a select committee, on which he himself ultimately served together with Benjamin Barton, Dr. Caspar Wistar, and others, was carried. This committee was "to collect materials for forming the natural history of the Hessian fly, and the best means for its prevention or destruction."[11] This pest is now combated in Albemarle County by late plantings and rotations. A later example of Jefferson's desire to extend the benefits of agricultural improvements is to be found in connection with his Merino sheep. In 1810, he proposed to another sheep enthusiast, President Madison, that they distribute their full-blooded males, one to a county throughout the State, a process which would take about seven years, encouraging formation in each county of small societies to maintain and provide rules for the use of the rams.

FARM MANAGEMENT AND OPERATIONS

During the short period following his retirement as Secretary of State, Jefferson threw his energies into farming operations. A summer visitor, Rochefoucauld, described him superintending the harvest. This description is one of the few real pictures which we have of Jefferson personally engaged in farming operations. It is probable, however, that Jefferson's participation in the actual manual tasks of farming was very slight. The size of his estates and the labor situation were such as to call, primarily, for managerial ability. This does not mean that he did not work with his hands. Apparently he had a basement workshop, and his manager, Edmund Bacon, described him at work on various models in which he was interested. Among agricultural implements these included the seed drill, the hemp brake, and the threshing machine. Of the various mechanical improvements which he made, none, it is probable, illustrates Jefferson's ability as a craftsman more clearly than the development of the improved moldboard for a plow.

THE MOLDBOARD FOR THE PLOW

The design and working principles of this moldboard which, in Jefferson's words, combine "a *theory* which may satisfy the learned, with a *practice* intelligible to the

---

[10] Jefferson to William Drayton, from Paris, May 6, 1786. See p. 72-73.
[11] American Philosophical Society, *Early Proceedings*, 22:193 (Philadelphia, 1883).

most unlettered labourer,"[12] engaged Jefferson's mind from time to time for more than a quarter of a century. The moldboard is first mentioned in his notes on a trip he made from the Rhine to Paris in April 1788. Observing the clumsy peasant ox plows along the way, he sketched a block of wood which, when cut according to specifications, constituted a moldboard that would raise and turn soil more efficiently. Before using the term "least resistance" in his paper, presented to the American Philosophical Society in May 1798, he read William Emerson, the English mathematician, and consulted with his fellow Society members, the American mathematicians, David Rittenhouse and Robert Patterson, professor of mathematics at the University of Pennsylvania.

Simplicity of construction is a keypoint of the contribution. Improved moldboards had been made by various persons, as Jefferson undoubtedly was well aware, but these were too complicated for the great mass of farmers, who continued, in shaping their implements, to follow methods such as those of the old Saxons. Plows had iron points, but when the moldboard split, the plowman cut out a section of a tree, judged the grain, and adzed it roughly into shape. Sometimes the result was efficient. Sometimes it was not. What Jefferson supplied was a simple formula whereby the husbandman could, with two common implements — the saw and the adze — construct a moldboard, which, considering both implements and methods, would operate to the greatest advantage or offer "the least resistance." Modifications of the board made by Jefferson and others subsequently appeared. Thus Valencienne on the staff of the Paris Museum of Natural History reproduced Jefferson's drawings in perspective, and a diagram of what may be termed the Jefferson-Valencienne model to fit the French plow appears in the Museum's *Annales* for 1802.

When viewed in perspective from the technical standpoint, as a contribution to the development of agricultural engineering, Jefferson's moldboard represents, I believe, if a line of distinction be drawn, the last great fundamental development in the series of wooden plows, the product of the family farm rather than the first great development in the series of present-day metal plows. This, together with the fact that in accord with his philosophy of agricultural improvement, as explained to Charles Willson Peale in 1815, he took out no patent, is perhaps a basic reason for small recognition by writers of the machine age of the importance of his effort. From the cultural standpoint Jefferson's description had far-reaching consequences. Its publication in the United States, France, and Great Britain centered attention upon the plow and the necessity for further efforts toward its improvement. The moldboard of the Paris Museum of Natural History was placed among the museum's agricultural exhibits as a study aid in the course of agricultural education. In this the French were, perhaps, a little ahead of the United States, but, on July 9, 1805, the Jefferson moldboard was exhibited at a meeting of the Philadelphia Society for the Promotion of Agriculture in Philosophical Hall of the College of Physicians. After the meeting this moldboard was probably used for practical purposes. That was one hundred and thirty-eight years ago, and, so far as is known, no Jefferson moldboard, other than the one just made at the United States Department of Agriculture, exists today in any agricultural exhibit either in this country or abroad.

Jefferson in 1798 had written Sir John Sinclair of the British Board of Agriculture that he planned to cast his moldboard in iron, but the credit for this practice in the United States goes to others. Jethro Wood, encouraged by Jefferson,

---

[12] Jefferson to Sir John Sinclair, from Philadelphia, Mar. 23, 1798. See p. 40-44.

produced a moldboard representing significantly in his words, "a sort of plano-curvilinear" figure. Wood's plow, however, worked badly in the heavy western soils, which clung to its pitted surface. Sometimes the large wooden plow was preferred to the metal, until after 1837 when the John Deere plow came into production. One of these plows, made in 1838 from a broken circular saw blade, is now on exhibition at the United States National Museum. In the forties, a factory was established in Moline, Illinois, and a few years later the prairie farmers were buying thousands yearly. Bright steel scouring, this plow served to break the plains of the vast area of the Louisiana Purchase, today's food arsenal for freedom-inspired fighting populations throughout the world.

SOIL CONSERVATION AND CONTOUR PLOWING

Down the sides and slopes of the Appalachians and the great Mississippi Basin run each year, in war and peace, the tiny rivulets, silting the waterways and draining away the Nation's resources to the deltas at the rivers' mouths. Nature's work of a thousand years may go in a night. Erosion is a problem as old as civilization. The Romans knew it. The Old World knew it; and Jefferson and his neighbors knew and feared its consequences on the soils of Albemarle. Those who have examined Jefferson's accounts know that in the latter part of his life he was deep in debt. This, it would be difficult to maintain, was a consequence of his inability in any particular field. Rather, it was the result of a combination of circumstances, important among which were the long periods of public service when he had to leave Monticello to the care of managers. Another circumstance was the red soils of his estate which quickly gullied and washed away to the disadvantage of its owner. Thus, in 1794, he wrote Washington that a careful examination of his lands had disclosed that "ten years' abandonment of them to the ravages of overseers, has brought on them a degree of degradation far beyond what I had expected."[13] The staples, tobacco and corn, both clean-tilled crops, contributed to both soil washing and soil exhaustion. At this time, Jefferson worked out and put into effect a system of rotations employing legumes, concerning which he corresponded at length with John Taylor of Caroline County. Fifteen years later, on his retirement from the Presidency, he was again free to fight gullies and employ his knowledge of soils by the use of gypsum and contour plowing.

Where Jefferson learned such plowing is not known. Its origins are as old as we have records, and he may have read its description in his library volume of Columella or seen it practiced on the slopes of Europe. What is important is that his was the first great voice in the United States to urge its practice. Following this practice with the aid of a hillside plow designed by his son-in-law, Thomas Mann Randolph, together with the use of plaster and clover, he hoped to restore again the fertility of the soil which once he said was "exceeded by no upland in the state."[14]

Jefferson, in this, was one hundred years ahead of his time. When so much good cheap land existed, the difficulties of spreading a conservation message were large. Changing agricultural practices is changing a way of life. Slow and constant long-time pressure is needed. Some of Jefferson's neighbors practiced contour plowing, but despite constant preachment by many leaders it was not widely taken up until recent

---

[13] Jefferson to George Washington, from Monticello, May 14, 1794. See p. 45-46.
[14] Jefferson to Tristam Dalton, from Monticello, May 2, 1817. See p. 46-47.

years. Soil conservation is not the work of the individual. It is a community matter calling for neighborhood help. Since establishment of the Soil Conservation Service in 1935, State laws have provided for 850 soil conservation districts throughout the United States. In and about Albemarle is the Thomas Jefferson Soil Conservation District. Operating on Jeffersonian democratic principles, the members of such districts formulate their own conservation ordinances in the same way that a town may pass ordinances for its own protection. These soil conservation ordinances have the force and effect of law, and the will of the majority now sets forms of land use and cultivation such as those once practiced by Jefferson.

AGRICULTURAL SOCIETIES

A small beginning in neighborly agricultural cooperation occurred in 1817, when Jefferson's friends and neighbors - statesmen, lawyers, and farmers - met together in Charlottesville to form the Albemarle County Agricultural Society. Agricultural societies for mutual aid and study of technical problems go back to the Roman Empire, and in this country the American Philosophical Society and the Philadelphia Society for the Promotion of Agriculture brought forth a great progeny. The Albemarle Society, primarily local, had many objectives as penned by Jefferson. Attention was to be given to production of staples including wheat, tobacco, and hemp, to soil improvement, the care of livestock, the development of farm machinery, and the "destruction of noxious quadrupeds, fowls, insects, and reptiles." Jefferson regarded the regular filling out of report forms by members as very important. Both good and bad practices were to be reported, the former for imitation, the latter for avoidance. "The choicest processes culled from every farm," he believed, "would compose a course probably near perfection."[15]

Under the presidency of James Madison and others the Society prospered. Thomas Mann Randolph, Jefferson's son-in-law, and Thomas Jefferson Randolph, his grandson, were members. Steps were taken for the establishment of a nursery and a Society machinery headquarters. Efforts were made to improve the breed of local livestock, and premiums were offered for crop production and farm implement improvement. Preoccupation with the University probably explains Jefferson's singular personal inactivity in the affairs of this Society, but a resolution offered by his fellow conservationist, General John H. Cocke, in 1822, called for the use of $1,000 in the hands of the treasurer to start a fund for the maintenance of a professor of agriculture at the University of Virginia. In its view that this professorship would "hasten and perpetuate the march of Agricultural improvement already so happily commenced,"[16] the Society was expressing a deep-lying sentiment of its founding spirit. Many other local societies and organizations drew inspiration from the words and writings of Jefferson, and, when, in observance of the seventy-fifth anniversary of the establishment of the Land-Grant College System and the United States Department of Agriculture, a wreath, composed of plants produced by genetical science, was placed at Monticello, the societies and farm organizations were represented among those paying homage.

---

[15] Jefferson's "Scheme for a System of Agricultural Societies, March 1811." See p. 75-77. Cf. Rodney H. True, ed., "Minute Book of the Agricultural Society of Albemarle," American Historical Association, *Annual Report*, 1918, 1:264-265 (Washington, 1921).

[16] True, "Minute Book of the Agricultural Society of Albemarle," 298.

AGRICULTURAL EDUCATION

For many years Jefferson had urged the teaching of agriculture, coupled with a thorough grounding in the attendant sciences, in institutions of higher learning. In 1803, noting a drift from the land, he wrote to David Williams on the importance of the establishment of a professorship of agriculture in "every" college and university. "Young men," he believed, "closing their academical education with this, as the crown of all other sciences, fascinated with its solid charms, and at a time when they are to choose an occupation, instead of crowding the other classes, would return to the farms of their fathers, their own, or those of others, and replenish and invigorate a calling, now languishing under contempt and oppression."[17] In that year, in his first plan for the University of Virginia, he noted agriculture, botany, and chemistry among the subjects to be taught. These same subjects are specified to be taught at the University in his draft of a bill for establishing a system of public education, dated 1817. In 1824, an enactment of the Board of Visitors for the organization of the University, Jefferson being present, provided that botany, chemistry, and rural economy should be taught in the school of natural history. In 1826, he wrote to the newly appointed professor of natural history, suggesting that rural economy might be taught by "seasonable alliances with the kindred subjects of Chemistry, Botany and Zoology."[18] Jefferson's advanced concept of scientific agricultural education was first realized in the West when, in the 1850s, a college of agriculture was established in Michigan. Then, in 1862, came the Land-Grant College Act which made it possible for each State to establish agricultural colleges staffed with competent faculties and specialists in the many sciences recognized as fundamental to the earth's full harvest.

THE LIVING JEFFERSON

In this year of Jefferson's bicentenary, a joint resolution was introduced in Congress providing for the appointment of the National Agricultural Jefferson Bicentenary Committee to carry out, under the general direction of the United States Commission for the Celebration of the Two-Hundredth Anniversary of the Birth of Thomas Jefferson, appropriate exercises and activities in recognition of his services and contributions to the farmers and the agriculture of the Nation. This resolution, after citing Jefferson's services as the patriotic statesman and philosopher, the author of the Declaration of Independence, the citizen of Virginia, and President of the United States, tells of his work as the farmer, the father of scientific agriculture, the conservationist, and the advocate of agricultural education. "As a figure, against the background of the soil of the land he loved," and here I am quoting from the resolution, "he stands as a symbol of its values, democracy and freedom, for the preservation of which the American farmers and all connected with the industry of agriculture are now contributing their maximum effort."[19] He remains, as the one of whom the Psalmist sang, "like a tree planted by the rivers of water, that bringeth forth his fruit in his season."[20]

---

[17] Jefferson to David Williams, from Washington, D. C., Nov. 14, 1803. See p. 81-82.

[18] Jefferson to John P. Emmett, from Monticello, May 2, 1826. See p. 83-84.

[19] U. S. Congress, 78 Congress, 1 Session, Joint Resolution Providing for the Appointment of a National Agricultural Jefferson Bicentenary Committee to Carry out under the General Direction of the United States Commission for the Celebration of the Birth of Thomas Jefferson appropriate Exercises and Activities in Recognition of His Services and Contributions to the Farmers and the Agriculture of the Nation, April 12, 1943, p. 3.

[20] Psalms, 1:3.

PART II

SELECTIONS FROM JEFFERSON'S WRITINGS

JEFFERSON'S VIEWS ON THE NATURE OF THE NATIONAL ECONOMY

From ancient times, statesmen have emphasized agriculture as the fundamental basis of national well-being, and, in consequence, the literature of the world is replete with eminent passages in praise of husbandry as the most satisfying and virtuous way of life.[1] In his early public career, Jefferson adhered emphatically to this view. Later, however, he sought an equilibrium of agriculture, manufactures, and commerce, and the following selections from his writings are presented to delineate the evolution of his views on the nature of the national economy.

FARMERS ARE GOD'S CHOSEN PEOPLE

The political economists of Europe have established it as a principle, that every State should endeavor to manufacture for itself; and this principle, like many others, we transfer to America, without calculating the difference of circumstance which should often produce a difference of result. In Europe the lands are either cultivated, or locked up against the cultivator. Manufacture must therefore be resorted to of necessity not of choice, to support the surplus of their people. But we have an immensity of land courting the industry of the husbandman. Is it best then that all our citizens should be employed in its improvement, or that one half should be called off from that to exercise manufactures and handicraft arts for the other? Those who labor in the earth are the chosen people of God, if ever He had a chosen people, whose breasts He has made His peculiar deposit for substantial and genuine virtue. It is the focus in which He keeps alive that sacred fire, which otherwise might escape from the face of the earth. Corruption of morals in the mass of cultivators is a phenomenon of which no age nor nation has furnished an example. It is the mark set on those, who, not looking up to heaven, to their own soil and industry, as does the husbandman, for their subsistence, depend for it on casualties and caprice of customers. Dependence begets subservience and venality, suffocates the germ of virtue, and prepares fit tools for the designs of ambition. This, the natural progress and consequence of the arts, has sometimes perhaps been retarded by accidental circumstances; but, generally speaking, the proportion which the aggregate of the other classes of citizens bears in any State to that of its husbandmen, is the proportion of its unsound to its healthy parts, and is a good enough barometer whereby to measure its degree of corruption. While we have land to labor then, let us never wish to see our citizens occupied at a workbench, or twirling a distaff. Carpenters, masons, smiths, are wanting in husbandry; but, for the general operations of manufacture, let our workshops remain in Europe. It is better to carry provisions and materials to workmen there, than bring them to the provisions and materials, and with them their manners and principles. The loss by the transportation of commodities across the Atlantic will be made up in happiness and permanence of government. The mobs of great cities add just so much to the support of pure

---

[1] Paul H. Johnstone, "In Praise of Husbandry," *Agricultural History*, 11:80-95 (April 1937), and "Turnips and Romanticism," *ibid.*, 12:224-255 (July 1938).

government, as sores do to the strength of the human body. It is the manners and spirit of a people which preserve a republic in vigor. A degeneracy in these is a canker which soon eats to the heart of its laws and constitution.[2]

ADVANTAGES OF AN AGRICULTURAL ECONOMY

I shall sometimes ask your permission to write you letters, not official, but private. The present is of this kind, and is occasioned by the question proposed in yours of June the 14th; "whether it would be useful to us, to carry all our own productions, or none?"

Were we perfectly free to decide this question, I should reason as follows. We have now lands enough to employ an infinite number of people in their cultivation. Cultivators of the earth are the most valuable citizens. They are the most vigorous, the most independent, the most virtuous, and they are tied to their country, and wedded to its liberty and interests, by the most lasting bonds. As long, therefore, as they can find employment in this line, I would not convert them into mariners, artisans, or anything else. But our citizens will find employment in this line, till their numbers, and of course their productions, become too great for the demand, both internal and foreign. This is not the case as yet, and probably will not be for a considerable time. As soon as it is, the surplus of hands must be turned to something else. I should then, perhaps, wish to turn them to the sea in preference to manufactures; because, comparing the characters of the two classes, I find the former the most valuable citizens. I consider the class of artificers as the panders of vice, and the instruments by which the liberties of a country are generally overturned. However, we are not free to decide this question on principles of theory only. Our people are decided in the opinion, that it is necessary for us to take a share in the occupation of the ocean, and their established habits induce them to require that the sea be kept open to them, and that that line of policy be pursued, which will render the use of that element to them as great as possible. I think it a duty in those entrusted with the administration of their affairs, to conform themselves to the decided choice of their constituents; and that therefore, we should, in every instance, preserve an equality of right to them in the transportation of commodities, in the right of fishing, and in the other uses of the sea.

But what will be the consequence? Frequent wars without a doubt. Their property will be violated on the sea, and in foreign ports, their persons will be insulted,

---

[2] Jefferson's *Notes on Virginia*, in Paul Leicester Ford, ed., *The Writings of Thomas Jefferson*, 3:268-269 (10 vols., New York, 1892-1899). Hereafter, this edition is cited as the Ford edition. Also in Andrew A. Lipscomb and Albert Ellery Bergh, eds., *The Writings of Thomas Jefferson*, 2:228-230 (20 vols., Washington, D. C., 1904-05). Hereafter, this edition is referred to as the Lipscomb and Bergh edition. Also in H. A. Washington, ed., *The Writings of Thomas Jefferson*, 8:404-406 (Washington, D. C., 1854). Hereafter, this edition is cited as the Washington edition.

Jefferson compiled his *Notes on Virginia* in 1781. It has been described by G. Brown Goode of the Smithsonian Institution as "the first comprehensive treatise upon the topography, natural history and natural resources of one of the United States, and was the precursor of the great library of scientific reports which have since been issued by the State and Federal governments. Though hastily prepared to meet a special need, if measured by its influence it is the most important scientific work as yet published in America."—Lipscomb and Bergh ed., 19:iv. For discussions on the history, nature, and importance of the *Notes on Virginia*, see Ralph H. Brown, "Jefferson's Notes on Virginia," *Geographical Review*, 33:467-473 (July 1943); and Paul Leicester Ford, "Jefferson's Notes on Virginia," *Nation*, 58:80-81, 98-99 (Feb. 1, 8, 1894).

imprisoned, &c., for pretended debts, contracts, crimes, contraband, &c., &c. These insults must be resented, even if we had no feelings, yet to prevent their eternal repetition; or, in other words, our commerce on the ocean and in other countries, must be paid for by frequent war. The justest dispositions possible in ourselves, will not secure us against it. It would be necessary that all other nations were just also. Justice indeed, on our part, will save us from those wars which would have been produced by a contrary disposition. But how can we prevent those produced by the wrongs of other nations? By putting ourselves in a condition to punish them. Weakness provokes insult and injury, while a condition to punish, often prevents them. This reasoning leads to the necessity of some naval force; that being the only weapon by which we can reach an enemy. I think it to our interest to punish the first insult; because an insult unpunished is the parent of many others. We are not, at this moment, in a condition to do it, but we should put ourselves into it, as soon as possible. . . .[3]

THE PLACE OF COMMERCE

. . . . You ask what I think on the expediency of encouraging our States to be commercial? Were I to indulge my own theory, I should wish them to practice neither commerce nor navigation, but to stand, with respect to Europe, precisely on the footing of China. We should thus avoid wars, and all our citizens would be husbandmen. Whenever, indeed, our numbers should so increase as that our produce would overstock the markets of those nations who should come to seek it, the farmers must either employ the surplus of their time in manufactures, or the surplus of our hands must be employed in manufactures or in navigation. But that day would, I think, be distant, and we should long keep our workmen in Europe, while Europe should be drawing rough materials, and even subsistence from America. But this is theory only, and a theory which the servants of America are not at liberty to follow. Our people have a decided taste for navigation and commerce. They take this from their mother country; and their servants are in duty bound to calculate all their measures on this datum: we wish to do it by throwing open all the doors of commerce, and knocking off its shackles. But as this cannot be done for others, unless they will do it for us, and there is no great probability that Europe will do this, I suppose we shall be obliged to adopt a system which may shackle them in our ports, as they do us in theirs. . . .[4]

AGRICULTURE AS THE SOURCE OF VIRTUE, FREEDOM, AND HAPPINESS

I have read with very great satisfaction the sheets of your work on the commerce of France and the United States, which you were so good as to put into my hands. I think you treat the subject, as far as these sheets go, in an excellent manner. Were I to select any particular passages as giving me particular satisfaction, it would be those wherein you prove to the United States that they will be more virtuous, more

---

[3] Jefferson to John Jay, from Paris, Aug. 23, 1785, in Ford ed., 4:87-90; Lipscomb and Bergh ed., 5:93-96; and Washington ed., 1:403-405.
[4] Jefferson to Count Gysbert-Charles van Hogendorp, from Paris, Oct. 13, 1785. For the complete letter, see Ford ed., 4:102-106; Lipscomb and Bergh ed., 5:180-184; and Washington ed., 1:463-466.

free, and more happy, employed in agriculture, than as carriers or manufacturers. It is a truth, and a precious one for them, if they could be persuaded of it. . . .[5]

THE DANGERS OF URBANIZATION

. . . . After all, it is my principle that the will of the majority should always prevail. If they approve the proposed Convention in all its parts, I shall concur in it cheerfully, in hopes that they will amend it whenever they shall find it works wrong. I think our governments will remain virtuous for many centuries; as long as they are chiefly agricultural; and this will be as long as there shall be vacant lands in any part of America. When they get piled upon one another in large cities, as in Europe, they will become corrupt as in Europe. Above all things I hope the education of the common people will be attended to; convinced that on their good sense we may rely with the most security for the preservation of a due degree of liberty. I have tired you by this time with my disquisitions & will therefore only add assurances of the sincerity of those sentiments of esteem & attachment with which I am Dear Sir your affectionate friend & servant.[6]

THE FRONTIER AS A SAFETY-VALVE[7]

. . . . As yet our manufacturers are as much at their ease, as independent and moral as our agricultural inhabitants, and they will continue so as long as there are vacant lands for them to resort to; because whenever it shall be attempted by the other classes to reduce them to the minimum of subsistence, they will quit their trades and go to laboring the earth. A first question is, whether it is desirable for us to receive at present the dissolute and demoralized handicraftsmen of the old cities of Europe? A second and more difficult one is, when even good handicraftsmen arrive here, is it better for them to set up their trade, or go to the culture of the earth? Whether their labor in their trade is worth more than their labor on the soil, increased by the creative energies of the earth? Had I time to revise that chapter,[8] this question should be discussed, and other views of the subject taken, which are presented by the wonderful changes which have taken place here since 1781, when the Notes on Virginia were written. Perhaps when I retire, I may amuse myself with a serious review of this work; at present it is out of the question. Accept my salutations and good wishes.[9]

---

[5] Jefferson to Jean Pierre Brissot de Warville, from Paris, Aug. 16, 1786, in Ford ed., 4:280-283; Lipscomb and Bergh ed., 5:402-404; and Washington ed., 2:11-13.

[6] Jefferson to James Madison, from Paris, Dec. 20, 1787. The text here used is from the Ford ed., 4:473-480. See also Lipscomb and Bergh ed., 6:385-393; and Washington ed., 2:327-333. The first part of the letter consists of a long discussion on various features of the newly drafted Constitution.

[7] During the last fifty years, considerable emphasis has been placed on the frontier as an influence in the development of the United States. The starting point of this emphasis is Frederick Jackson Turner's famous essay on "The Significance of the Frontier in American History (1893)." For the literature on the subject, see Everett E. Edwards, "References on the Significance of the Frontier in American History," U. S. Department of Agriculture, *Bibliographical Contributions 25* (ed. 2, Washington, 1939). Turner, however, had precursors, including Jefferson, and the letter from Jefferson to J. Lithgow is, therefore, of unusual interest.

[8] The reference is to ch. 19 of Jefferson's *Notes on Virginia*.

[9] Jefferson to J. Lithgow, from Washington, D. C., Jan. 4, 1805, in Ford ed., 3:79, 269-270; Lipscomb and Bergh ed., 11:55-56; and Washington ed., 4:563-564.

THE PLACE OF MANUFACTURING

. . . . I have lately inculcated the encouragement of manufactures to the extent of our own consumption at least, in all articles of which we raise the raw material. On this the federal papers and meetings have sounded the alarm of Chinese policy, destruction of commerce, &c.; that is to say, the iron which we make must not be wrought here into ploughs, axes, hoes, &c., in order that the ship-owner may have the profit of carrying it to Europe, and bringing it back in a manufactured form, as if after manufacturing our own raw materials for own use, there would not be a surplus produce sufficient to employ a due proportion of navigation in carrying it to market and exchanging it for those articles of which we have not the raw material. Yet this absurd hue and cry has contributed much to federalize New England, their doctrine goes to the sacrificing agriculture and manufactures to commerce; to the calling all our people from the interior country to the sea-shore to turn merchants, and to convert this great agricultural country into a city of Amsterdam. But I trust the good sense of our country will see that its greatest prosperity depends on a due balance between agriculture, manufactures and commerce, and not in this protuberant navigation which has kept us in hot water from the commencement of our government, and is now engaging us in war. That this may be avoided, if it can be done without a surrender of rights, is my sincere prayer. Accept the assurances of my constant esteem and respect.[10]

. . . . You tell me I am quoted by those who wish to continue our dependence on England for manufactures. There was a time when I might have been so quoted with more candor, but within the thirty years which have since elapsed, how are circumstances changed! We were then in peace. Our independent place among nations was acknowledged. A commerce which offered the raw material in exchange for the same material after receiving the last touch of industry, was worthy of welcome to all nations. It was expected that those especially to whom manufacturing industry was important, would cherish the friendship of such customers by every favor, by every inducement, and particularly cultivate their peace by every act of justice and friendship. Under this prospect the question seemed legitimate, whether, with such an immensity of unimproved land, courting the hand of husbandry, the industry of agriculture, or that of manufactures, would add most to the national wealth? And the doubt was entertained on this consideration chiefly, that to the labor of the husbandman a vast addition is made by the spontaneous energies of the earth on which it is employed: for one grain of wheat committed to the earth, she renders twenty, thirty, and even fifty fold, whereas to the labor of the manufacturer nothing is added. Pounds of flax, in his hands, yield, on the contrary, but pennyweights of lace. This exchange, too, laborious as it might seem, what a field did it promise for the occupations of the ocean; what a nursery for that class of citizens who were to exercise and maintain our equal rights on that element? This was the state of things in 1785, when the "Notes on Virginia" were first printed; when, the ocean being open to all nations, and their common right in it acknowledged and exercised under regulations sanctioned by the assent and usage of all, it was thought that the doubt might claim some consideration. But who in 1785 could foresee the rapid depravity which was to render the close of that century the disgrace of the history of man? . . . We must now place the manufacturer by the side of the agriculturist. . . .

---

[10]Jefferson to Thomas Leiper, from Washington, D. C., Jan. 21, 1809. For the complete letter, see Ford ed., 9: 238-239; Lipscomb and Bergh ed., 12: 236-238; and Washington ed., 5: 416-418.

experience has taught me that manufactures are now as necessary to our independence as to our comfort; and if those who quote me as of a different opinion, will keep pace with me in purchasing nothing foreign where an equivalent of domestic fabric can be obtained, without regard to difference of price, it will not be our fault if we do not soon have a supply at home equal to our demand, and wrest that weapon of distress from the hand which has wielded it. . . . [11]

EQUILIBRIUM OF AGRICULTURE, MANUFACTURES, AND COMMERCE

. . . . An equilibrium of agriculture, manufactures, and commerce, is certainly become essential to our independence. Manufactures, sufficient for our own consumption, of what we raise the raw material (and no more). Commerce sufficient to carry the surplus produce of agriculture, beyond our own consumption, to a market for exchanging it for articles we cannot raise (and no more). These are the true limits of manufactures and commerce. To go beyond them is to increase our dependence on foreign nations, and our liability to war.

These three important branches of human industry will then grow together, and be really handmaids to each other. I salute you with great respect and esteem. [12]

---

[11] Jefferson to Benjamin Austin, from Monticello, Jan. 9, 1816. For complete letter, see Ford ed., 10:7-11; Lipscomb and Bergh ed., 14:387-393; and Washington ed., 6:520-523.
[12] Jefferson to John Jay, from Monticello, Apr. 7, 1809, in Lipscomb and Bergh ed., 12:270-271; and Washington ed., 5:440.

JEFFERSON'S OBSERVATIONS ON AGRICULTURE IN EUROPE AND THE UNITED STATES

Jefferson traveled widely and manifested a keen interest in farming conditions and methods wherever he went. The following selections from his writings are presented to show his capacities as an observer and reporter. In essence, however, they also provide a survey of actual agricultural conditions during Jefferson's lifetime.

ENGLISH AGRICULTURE

. . . . I returned but three or four days ago from a two months' trip to England. I traversed that country much, and own both town and country fell short of my expectations. Comparing it with this, I found a much greater proportion of barrens, a soil, in other parts, not naturally so good as this, not better cultivated, but better manured, and, therefore, more productive. This proceeds from the practice of long leases there, and short ones here. The laboring people here are poorer than in England. They pay about one half their produce in rent; the English, in general, about a third. The gardening, in that country, is the article in which it surpasses all the earth. I mean their pleasure gardening. This, indeed, went far beyond my ideas. The city of London, though handsomer than Paris, is not so handsome as Philadelphia. Their architecture is in the most wretched style I ever saw, not meaning to except America, where it is bad, nor even Virginia, where it is worse than in any other part of America which I have seen. . . . In the arts, the most striking thing I saw there, new, was the application of the principle of the steam engine to grist mills. I saw eight pair of stones which are worked by steam, and there are to be set up thirty pair in the same house. A hundred bushels of coal a day, are consumed at present. I do not know in what proportion the consumption will be increased by the additional geer. . . . [13]

FRENCH AGRICULTURE

. . . . I am constantly roving about, to see what I have never seen before, and shall never see again. In the great cities, I go to see what travellers think alone worthy of being seen; but I make a job of it, and generally gulp it all down in a day. On the other hand, I am never satiated with rambling through the fields and farms, examining the culture and cultivators, with a degree of curiosity which makes some take me to be a fool, and others to be much wiser than I am. I have been pleased to find among the people a less degree of physical misery than I had expected. They are generally well clothed, and have a plenty of food, not animal indeed, but vegetable, which is as wholesome. Perhaps they are over-worked, the excess of the rent required by the landlord obliging them to too many hours of labor in order to produce that, and wherewith to feed and clothe themselves. The soil of Champagne and Burgundy I have found more universally good than I had expected, and as I could not help making a comparison with England, I found that comparison more unfavorable to the latter than is generally admitted. The soil, the climate, and the productions are superior to those

---

[13] Jefferson to John Page, from Paris, May 4, 1786. For the complete letter, see Ford ed., 4: 212-215; Lipscomb and Bergh ed., 5: 303-306; and Washington ed., 1: 548-551.

of England, and the husbandry as good, except in one point; that of manure. In England, long leases for twenty-one years, or three lives, to wit, that of the farmer, his wife, and son, renewed by the son as soon as he comes to the possession, for his own life, his wife's and eldest child's, and so on, render the farms there almost hereditary, make it worth the farmer's while to manure the lands highly, and give the landlord an opportunity of occasionally making his rent keep pace with the improved state of the lands. Here the leases are either during pleasure, or for three, six, or nine years, which does not give the farmer time to repay himself for the expensive operation of well manuring, and, therefore, he manures ill, or not at all. I suppose, that could the practice of leasing for three lives be introduced in the whole kingdom, it would, within the term of your life, increase agricultural productions fifty per cent.; or were any one proprietor to do it with his own lands, it would increase his rents fifty per cent., in the course of twenty-five years. But I am told the laws do not permit it. The laws then, in this particular, are unwise and unjust, and ought to give that permission. In the southern provinces, where the soil is poor, the climate hot and dry, and there are few animals, they would learn the art, found so precious in England, of making vegetable manure, and thus improving these provinces in the article in which nature has been least kind to them. Indeed, these provinces afford a singular spectacle. Calculating on the poverty of their soil, and their climate by its latitude only, they should have been the poorest in France. On the contrary, they are the richest, from one fortuitous circumstance. Spurs or ramifications of high mountains, making down from the Alps, and, as it were, reticulating these provinces, give to the valleys the protection of a particular inclosure to each, and the benefit of a general stagnation of the northern winds produced by the whole of them, and thus countervail the advantage of several degrees of latitude. From the first olive fields of Pierrelatte, to the orangeries of Hieres, has been continued rapture to me. . . .

You will not wonder at the subjects of my letters; they are the only ones which have been presented to my mind for some time past; and the waters must always be what are the fountains from which they flow. . . .[14]

AGRICULTURE IN VIRGINIA

I should have taken time ere this to have considered the observations of Mr. [Arthur] Young, could I at this place have done it in such a way as would satisfy either him or myself. When I wrote the notes of the last year, I had never before thought of calculating what were the profits of a capital invested in Virginia agriculture. . . . Mr. Young must not pronounce too hastily on the impossibility of an annual production of £750 worth of wheat coupled with a cattle product of £125. My object was to state the produce of a *good* farm, under *good* husbandry as practiced in my part of the country. Manure does not enter into this, because we can buy an acre of new land cheaper than we can manure an old acre. Good husbandry with us consists in abandoning Indian corn and tobacco, tending small grain, some red clover following, and endeavoring to have, while the lands are at rest, a spontaneous cover of white clover. I do not present this as a culture judicious in itself, but as *good* in comparison with what most people there pursue. Mr. Young has never had an opportunity of seeing how slowly the fertility of the *original soil* is exhausted. With moderate management of it, I can

---

[14]Jefferson to Lafayette, from Nice, Apr. 11, 1787. For the complete letter, see Lipscomb and Bergh ed., 6: 106-110; and Washington ed., 2: 134-137.

affirm that the James river lowgrounds with the cultivation of small grain, will never be exhausted; because we know that under that cultivation we must now and then take them down with Indian corn, or they become, as they were originally, too rich to bring wheat. The highlands, where I live, have been cultivated about sixty years. The culture was tobacco and Indian corn as long as they would bring enough to pay the labor. Then they were turned out. After four or five years rest they would bring good corn again, and in double that time perhaps good tobacco. Then they would be exhausted by a second series of tobacco and corn. Latterly we have begun to cultivate small grain; and excluding Indian corn, and following, such of them as were originally good, soon rise up to fifteen or twenty bushels the acre. We allow that every laborer will manage ten acres of wheat, except at harvest. I have no doubt but the coupling cattle and sheep with this would prodigiously improve the produce. This improvement Mr. Young will be better able to calculate than anybody else. I am so well satisfied of it myself, that having engaged a good farmer from the head of Elk, (the style of farming there you know well,) I mean in a farm of about 500 acres of cleared land and with a dozen laborers to try the plan of wheat, rye, potatoes, clover, with a mixture of some Indian corn with the potatoes, and to push the number of sheep. This last hint I have taken from Mr. Young's letters which you have been so kind as to communicate to me. I have never before considered with due attention the profit from that animal. I shall not be able to put the farm into that form exactly the ensuing autumn, but against another I hope I shall, and I shall attend with precision to the measures of the ground and of the product, which may perhaps give you something hereafter to communicate to Mr. Young which may gratify him, but I will furnish the ensuing winter what was desired in Mr. Young's letter of Jan. 17, 1793. I have the honor to be, with great and sincere esteem, dear Sir, your most obedient humble servant.[15]

DIFFERENCES BETWEEN THE POLITICAL ECONOMY OF EUROPE AND AMERICA

.... The differences of circumstance between this and the old countries of Europe, furnish differences of fact whereon to reason, in questions of political economy, and will consequently produce sometimes a difference of result. There, for instance, the quantity of food is fixed, or increasing in a slow and only arithmetical ration, and the proportion is limited by the same ratio. Supernumerary births consequently add only to your mortality. Here the immense extent of uncultivated and fertile lands enables every one who will labor, to marry young, and to raise a family of any size. Our food, then, may increase geometrically with our laborers, and our births, however multiplied, become effective. Again, there the best distribution of labor is supposed to be that which places the manufacturing hands alongside the agricultural; so that the one part shall feed both, and the other part furnish both with clothes and other comforts. Would that be best here? Egoism and first appearances say yes. Or would it be better that all our laborers should be employed in agriculture? In this case a double or treble portion of fertile lands would be brought into culture; a double or treble

---

[15] Jefferson to President Washington, from Philadelphia, June 28, 1793, in Ford ed., 6:82-84; Lipscomb and Bergh ed., 9:139-143; and Washington ed., 4:3-5.
On Jan. 25, 1791, Arthur Young, the famous English agricultural writer, wrote to Washington, soliciting information with respect to the prices of lands, stock, grain, amount of taxes, &c. &c." in the United States. To meet this request, Washington sought data from "some of the most intelligent farmers in the State of New-York, New-Jersey, Pennsylvania, Maryland, and Virginia." Jefferson submitted "Notes on Mr. Young's Letter" on June 18, 1792, and then followed with the letter that is here reprinted. See *Letters from His Excellency George Washington to Arthur Young . . . and Sir John Sinclair . . .* (Alexandria, Va., 1803).

creation of food be produced, and its surplus go to nourish the now perishing births of Europe, who in return would manufacture and send us in exchange our clothes and other comforts. Morality listens to this, and so invariably do the laws of nature create our duties and interests, that when they seem to be at variance, we ought to suspect some fallacy in our reasonings. In solving this question, too, we should allow its just weight to the moral and physical preference of the agricultural, over the manufacturing, man. My occupations permit me only to ask questions. They deny me the time, if I had the information, to answer them. Perhaps, as worthy the attention of the author of the *Traité d'Economie Politique*, I shall find them answered in that work. If they are not, the reason will have been that you wrote for Europe; while I shall have asked them because I think for America. Accept, Sir, my respectful salutations, and assurances of great consideration.[16]

ALBEMARLE COUNTY, VIRGINIA

Your letter of June 15th came to hand in December, and it is not till the ratification of our peace, that a safe conveyance for an answer could be obtained. . . . The question proposed in my letter of February 1st, 1804, has since become quite a "question viseuse." I had then persuaded myself that a nation, distant as we are from the contentions of Europe, avoiding all offences to other powers, and not over-hasty in resenting offence from them, doing justice to all, faithfully fulfilling the duties of neutrality, performing all offices of amity, and administering to their interests by the benefits of our commerce, that such a nation, I say, might expect to live in peace, and consider itself merely as a member of the great family of mankind; that in such case it might devote itself to whatever it could best produce, secure of a peaceable exchange of surplus for what could be more advantageously furnished by others, as takes place between one county and another of France. But experience has shown that continued peace depends not merely on our own justice and prudence, but on that of others also; that when forced into war, the interception of exchanges which must be made across a wide ocean, becomes a powerful weapon in the hands of an enemy domineering over that element, and to the other distresses of war adds the want of all those necessaries for which we have permitted ourselves to be dependent on others, even arms and clothing. This fact, therefore, solves the question by reducing it to its ultimate form, whether profit or preservation is the first interest of a State? We are consequently become manufacturers to a degree incredible to those who do not see it, and who only consider the short period of time during which we have been driven to them by the suicidal policy of England. The prohibiting duties we lay on all articles of foreign manufacture which prudence requires us to establish at home, with the patriotic determination of every good citizen to use no foreign article which can be made within ourselves, without regard to difference of price, secures us against a relapse into foreign dependency. And this circumstance may be worthy of your consideration, should you continue in the disposition to emigrate to this country. Your manufactory of cotton, on a moderate scale combined with a farm, might be preferable to either singly, and the one or the other might become principal, as experience should recommend. Cotton ready spun is in ready demand, and if woven, still more so.

I will proceed now to answer the inquiries which respect your views of removal; and I am glad that, in looking over our map, your eye has been attracted by the village

---

[16]Jefferson to Jean Baptiste Say, from Washington, D. C., Feb. 1, 1804. For the complete letter, see Lipscomb and Bergh ed., 11: 1-3; and Washington ed., 4:526-527.

of Charlottesville, because I am better acquainted with that than any other portion of the United States, being within three or four miles of the place of my birth and residence. It is a portion of country which certainly possesses great advantages. Its soil is equal in natural fertility to any high lands I have ever seen; it is red and hilly, very like much of the country of Champagne and Burgundy, on the route of Sens, Vermanton, Vitteaux, Dijon, and along the Cote to Chagny, excellently adapted to wheat, maize, and clover; like all mountainous countries it is perfectly healthy, liable to no agues and fevers, or to any particular epidemic, as is evidenced by the robust constitution of its inhabitants, and their numerous families. As many instances of nonagenaires exist habitually in this neighborhood as in the same degree of population anywhere. Its temperature may be considered as a medium of that of the United States. . . . On an average of seven years I have found our snows amount in the whole to fifteen inches depth, and to cover the ground fifteen days; these, with the rains, give us four feet of water in the year. The garden pea, which we are now sowing, comes to table about the 12th of May; strawberries and cherries about the same time; asparagus the 1st of April. The artichoke stands the winter without cover; lettuce and endive with a slight one of bushes, and often without any; and the fig, protected by a little straw, begins to ripen in July; if unprotected, not till the 1st of September. There is navigation for boats of six tons from Charlottesville to Richmond, the nearest tidewater, and principal market for our produce. The country is what we call well inhabited, there being in our county, Albemarle, of about seven hundred and fifty square miles, about twenty thousand inhabitants, or twenty-seven to a square mile, of whom, however, one-half are people of color, either slaves or free. The society is much better than is common in country situations; perhaps there is not a better *country* society in the United States. But do not imagine this a Parisian or an academical society. It consists of plain, honest, and rational neighbors, some of them well informed and men of reading, all superintending their farms, hospitable and friendly, and speaking nothing but English. The manners of every nation are the standard of orthodoxy within itself. But these standards being arbitrary, reasonable people in all allow free toleration for the manners, as for the religion of others. Our culture is of wheat for market, and of maize, oats, peas, and clover, for the support of the farm. We reckon it a good distribution to divide a farm into three fields, putting one into wheat, half a one into maize, the other half into oats or peas, and the third into clover, and to tend the fields successively in this rotation. Some woodland in addition, is always necessary to furnish fuel, fences, and timber for constructions. Our best farmers (such as Mr. Randolph, my son-in-law) get from ten to twenty bushels of wheat to the acre; our worst (such as myself) from six to eighteen, with little or more manuring. The bushel of wheat is worth in common times about one dollar. The common produce of maize is from ten to twenty bushels, worth half a dollar the bushel, which is of a cubic foot and a quarter, or, more exactly, of two thousand one hundred and seventy-eight cubic inches. From these data you may judge best for yourself of the size of the farm which would suit your family: bearing in mind, that while you can be furnished by the farm itself for consumption, with every article it is adapted to produce, the sale of your wheat at market is to furnish the fund for all other necessary articles. I will add that both soil and climate are admirably adapted to the vine, which is the abundant natural production of our forests, and that you cannot bring a more valuable laborer than one acquainted with both its culture and manipulation into wine.

Your only inquiry now unanswered is, the price of these lands. To answer this with precision, would require details too long for a letter; the fact being, that we have no metallic measure of values at present, while we are overwhelmed with bank paper. The depreciation of this swells nominal prices, without furnishing any stable index of real value. . . . You may judge that, in this state of things, the holders of bank notes will give free prices for lands, and that were I to tell you simply the present prices of lands in this medium, it would give you no idea on which you could calculate. But I will state to you the progressive prices which have been paid for particular parcels of land for some years back, which may enable you to distinguish between the real increase of value regularly produced by our advancement in population, wealth, and skill, and the bloated value arising from the present disordered and dropsical state of our medium. There are two tracts of land adjoining me, and another not far off, all of excellent quality, which happen to have been sold at different epochs as follows:

One	was sold in	1793	for	$4	an acre,	in 1812,	at	$10,	and is now rated	$16.
The 2d	"	1786	"	5 1/3	"	1803	"	10,	"	20.
The 3d	"	1797	"	7	"	1811	"	16,	"	20.

On the whole, however, I suppose we may estimate that the steady annual rise of our lands is in a geometrical ratio of 5 per cent.; that were our medium now in a wholesome state, they might be estimated at from twelve to fifteen dollars the acre; and I may add, I believe with correctness, that there is not any part of the Atlantic States where lands of equal quality and advantages can be had as cheap. When sold with a dwelling-house on them, little additional is generally asked for the house. These buildings are generally of wooden materials, and of indifferent structure and accomodation. Most of the hired labor here is of people of color, either slaves or free. An able-bodied man has sixty dollars a year, and is clothed and fed by the employer; a woman half that. White laborers may be had, but they are less subordinate, their wages higher, and their nourishment much more expensive. A good horse for the plough costs fifty or sixty dollars. A draught ox twenty to twenty-five dollars. A milch cow fifteen to eighteen dollars. A sheep two dollars. Beef is about five cents, mutton and pork seven cents the pound. A turkey or goose fifty cents apiece, a chicken eight and one-third cents; a dozen eggs the same. Fresh butter twenty to twenty-five cents the pound. And, to render as full as I can, the information which may enable you to calculate for yourself, I enclose you a Philadelphia price-current, giving the prices in regular times of most of the articles of produce or manufacture, foreign and domestic.

That it may be for the benefit of your children and their descendants to remove to a country where, for enterprise and talents, so many avenues are open to fortune and fame, I have little doubt. But I should be afraid to affirm that, at your time of life, and with habits formed on the state of society in France, a change for one so entirely different would be for your personal happiness. Fearful, therefore, to persuade, I shall add with sincere truth, that I shall very highly estimate the addition of such a neighbor to our society, and that there is no service within my power which I shall not render with pleasure and promptitude. With this assurance be pleased to accept that of my great esteem and respect. . . .[17]

---

[17]Jefferson to Jean Baptiste Say, from Monticello, Mar. 2, 1815, in Lipscomb and Bergh ed., 14:258-267; and Washington ed., 6:430-436.

JEFFERSON'S FARMING ACTIVITIES

JEFFERSON'S LOVE OF FARMING

In spite of his many and varied interests, Jefferson always regarded himself as primarily a farmer, and assuredly one of his greatest delights was Monticello where he carried on extensive farming activities. The following letters—the first written while he was Secretary of State, the second and third after his return to Monticello, the fourth while he was still in the White House, and the fifth after his presidency—attest his love of farming.

I am going to Virginia. I have at length become able to fix that to the beginning of the new year. I am then to be liberated from the hated occupations of politics and to remain in the bosom of my family, my farm, and my books. I have my house to build [that is, remodeling Monticello], my fields to farm, and to watch for the happiness of those who labor for mine. I have one daughter married to a man of science, sense, virtue, and competence; in whom indeed I have nothing more to wish. They live with me. If the other [Maria] shall be as fortunate, in due process of time I shall imagine myself as blessed as the most blessed of the patriarchs.[18]

I am to thank you for the book you were so good as to transmit me, as well as the letter covering it, and your felicitations on my present quiet. The difference of my present and past situation is such as to leave me nothing to regret, but that my retirement has been postponed four years too long. The principles on which I calculated the value of life, are entirely in favor of my present course. I return to farming with an ardor which I scarcely knew in my youth, and which has got the better entirely of my love of study. Instead of writing ten or twelve letters a day, which I have been in the habit of doing as a thing in course, I put off answering my letters now, farmer-like, till a rainy day, and then find them sometimes postponed by other necessary occupations. . . . With wishes of every degree of happiness to you, both public and private, and with my best respects to Mrs. Adams, I am, your affectionate and humble servant.[19]

It was not in my power to attend at Fredericksburg according to the kind invitation in your letter, and in that of Mr. Ogilvie. The heat of the weather, the business of the farm, to which I have made myself necessary, forbade it; and to give one round reason for all, *mature sanus*, I have laid up my Rosinante in his stall, before his unfitness for the road shall expose him faultering to the world. But why did not I answer you in time? Because, in truth, I am encouraging myself to grow lazy, and I was sure you would ascribe the delay to anything sooner than a want of affection or respect

---

[18] Jefferson to Mrs. Angelica Church, from Germantown, Pa., Nov. 27, 1793. For the complete letter, see Ford ed., 6:454-456.
[19] Jefferson to Vice President Adams, from Monticello, Apr. 25, 1794, in Ford ed., 6:504-505; Lipscomb and Bergh ed., 9:283-284; and Washington ed., 4:103-104.

to you, for this was not among the possible causes. In truth, if anything could ever induce me to sleep another night out of my own house, it would have been your friendly invitation and my solicitude for the subject of it, the education of our youth. . . .[20]

. . . . At the end of my present term, of which two years are yet to come, I propose to retire from public life, and to close my days on my patrimony of Monticello, in the bosom of my family. I have hitherto enjoyed uniform health; but the weight of public business begins to be too heavy for me, and I long for the enjoyments of rural life, among my books, my farms and my family. Having performed my *quadragena stipendia*, I am entitled to my discharge, and should be sorry, indeed, that others should be sooner sensible than myself when I ought to ask it. . . .[21]

. . . . I have heard that you have retired from the city to a farm, and that you give your whole time to that. Does not the museum suffer? And is the farm as interesting? Here, as you know, we are all farmers, but not in a pleasing style. We have so little labor in proportion to our land that, although perhaps we make more profit from the same labor, we cannot give to our grounds that style of beauty which satisfies the eye of the amateur. Our rotations are corn, wheat, and clover, or corn, wheat, clover and clover, or wheat, corn, wheat, clover and clover, preceding the clover by a plastering. But some, instead of clover, substitute mere rest, and all are slovenly enough. We are adding the care of Merino sheep. I have often thought that if heaven had given me choice of my position and calling, it should have been on a rich spot of earth, well watered, and near a good market for the productions of the garden. No occupation is so delightful to me as the culture of the earth, and no culture comparable to that of the garden. Such a variety of subjects, some one always coming to perfection, the failure of one thing repaired by the success of another, and instead of one harvest a continued one through the year. Under a total want of demand except for our family table, I am still devoted to the garden. But though an old man, I am but a young gardener. . . .[22]

JEFFERSON'S FARM BOOK

Jefferson kept a Farm Book from 1774 to 1822, in which he recorded data about farming that he wished to remember. The volume, the original of which is in the Massachusetts Historical Society at Boston, supplies fragmentary but interesting sidelights on his farming activities, and the following excerpts from pages 82 and 87 are included here with the permission of the Society.

Dung

Folding. Mr Taylor says he knows by accurate & constant experience that 40. head of cattle, folded of nights only, dung completely 20. yds square.

---

[20] Jefferson to Mann Page, from Monticello, Aug. 30, 1795, in Ford ed., 7:23-25; Lipscomb and Bergh ed., 9:306-307; and Washington ed., 4:119-120. Rosinante was the name of Don Quixote's horse.

[21] Jefferson to Le Comte Diodati, from Washington, D. C., Mar. 29, 1807. For the complete letter, see Lipscomb and Bergh ed., 11:181-183; and Washington ed., 5:61-63.

[22] Jefferson to Charles Willson Peale, from Poplar Forest, Aug. 20, 1811. For the complete letter, see Lipscomb and Bergh ed., 13:78-80; and Washington ed., 6:6.

before folding the ground should be coultered & covered with straw, then folded one week, and the straw & dung immediately turned in with the great plough.

an Experiment to be tried. lay off a square acre & put 25 loads ₍yds₎ of dung on it. lay off 8 acres separately around it: fold 4 of them with a given number of cattle, & the other 4. with 5. or 6 times as many sheep, giving 1. week to one acre, 1½ to the 2d. 2 weeks to the 3d. & 2½ to the 4th. sow the whole with wheat, and see which of the folded acres is equal to the dunged one, in order to ascertain the equivalence between folding & spreading dung. . . .

Dung hill should be on a level, paved, with a well round it, shaded, channels at bottom to lead off superfluous moisture. . . .

Young sais that 20. head of sheep will fold 1. acre a year in a manner to equal 20. loads of dung. then the folding of one sheep a year is equivalent to one load of dung. 3. exp. yr. 166 This makes 20. sheep only equal to 1. cow. Mr Taylor's estimate in folding makes 1. cow fold 7/10 of an acre in a year. This makes 1. cow equal to 18. sheep.

Rotted dung. cattle, little & big, will make 10 loads ₍cubic yds₎ in 6. months if well littered. Logan. T. M. Randolph.

25. such loads serve to manure an acre. Logan.

it would be well worth while to confine & litter cattle in a yard thro' the summer. – Logan.

each head would then manure an acre a year.

dung is carried on in Dec. Jan. Feb.

Marle – an easy method of estimating accurately the quantity of calcareous earth they contain by dropping spirit of nitre till saturated, on that & on unburnt limestone. . . .

Gypsum a calcareous earth combined with a mineral acid. when the calcareous earth is predominent it is a good manure, when the 2. ingredients are balanced so as to neutralise it perfectly it is neither good nor bad. when the acid abounds it is injurious. . . .

Potatoes

planted alone in drills 5. f. apart, take 8. bushels of seed to the acre, if cut into eyes.

The unrotted dung of the last winter may be carried out in Mar. Apr. or May, & the potatoe furrow being made, & potatoes dropped in. This dung is then put over them, trodden in, & covered with a thin coat of earth. Mr Taylor thinks this much the most oeconomical way of using dung. it becomes well rotted & in a proper state for the succeeding crop of grain.

1795. Dec. Colo. N. Lewis', this year in drills 4 f. apart yielded 5 bush. to 140 yds. in the row = 130 bush. for a acre. he says a hand will dig 1/3 of an acre per day, say 43. bushels per day.

Young finds the planting at a foot apart all over the ground produce most & prepare the ground best for wheat. 3. Exp. yr. 260.

mixed with corn.

    one way is to drill the corn in 8.f. rows, & 18.I. apart in the row; then to drill the potatoes between. with good ploughing this is the best method. G. Washington.

    this method takes about 5. bushels of seed to the acre, if cut into eyes.

    Peters has tried this method many years, & measuring the produce of several acres it has been 40. bush. of corn & 120. bush. of potatoes to the acre.

    June is the best time for planting potatoes, by which time the corn may have been worked over 3 times. per Parker.

another way is to plant the corn & potatoes in 4.f. rows both ways, every other row being potatoes. This takes 2. or 2½ bush. of seed to the acre, &, with bad ploughmen, is the best, because of crop ploughing.

to feed with potatoes, they are put into a trough with some water, and stirred about with a switch broom, then put into a dry trough & chopped with an S, the blade of which is 7½ I long, 3 I. deep, & has a socket to receive the handle which is as long as a spade handle.

a double measure of potatoes yield as much nutriment as a single one of corn. Logan.

a peck of potatoes a day serves a horse. a handful of bran, or rye meal &c is mixed in for them.

a bushel a day serves a fattening ox.

JEFFERSON'S GARDEN BOOK

    The original of the Garden Book kept by Jefferson from 1766 to 1824 is also in the Massachusetts Historical Society at Boston. It provides ample testimony of his capacity for scientific discernment and of his deep interest in the processes of nature. The following excerpt describes the planting of grapevines on April 6, 1809.[23]

    Planted 30. [grape] vines just below where the new garden wall will run, towards the Westermost end. S of them at the Westermost end of the row were Spanish Raisins from Colo Bland's, next to them were 16. native vines from Winslow's in New Kent, and at the Easternmost end were 6. native vines of Monticello. They were planted by some Tuscan Vignerons who came over with Mr Mazzie. The manner was as follows.

---

[23]The excerpt is from p. 15-17 and is here printed with the permission of the Massachusetts Historical Society. For an account of the Garden Book, see Rodney H. True, "Thomas Jefferson's Garden Book," American Philosophical Society, *Proceedings*, 76:939-945 (1936).

A trench 4.f. deep and 4.f wide was dug. at the bottom were put small green bushes, and on them a thin coat of dung and earth mixed, which raised the bed to within 2½ feet of the surface. The cuttings which were from 3½ to 6.f. long, and which had been hitherto buried in the earth, were then produced, about 18.I. of their butts were dipt into a thick paste made of cowdung and water and then planted in the bottom, the Raisins 3.f. apart. The rest about 2.f. having a stick stuck by each to which it was bound with bear grass in order to support it while the earth should be drawn in. The earth was then thrown in, the mould first, and afterwards the other earth in the same order in which it was dug. leaving the bottom clay for the last. The earth was thrown in very loose & care was taken to avoid trampling in it. The trench was not quite filled, but left somewhat hollowing to receive & retain the water, & the superfluous earth was left on each side without the trench. Then the supporting sticks were drawn out and would have served for the other rows had the plantation been to be continued in such a case. The rows are to be 4 f. apart, so that in fact the whole surface is taken up to the depth of 4.f. The best way of doing it is to dig every other trench, and leave the earth which is thrown out exposed for a twelvemonth. Then the vines may be planted at any time from the middle of November to the first week in April afterwards dig the other alternate trenches, and leave the earth of these also exposed for a twelvemonth. when the latter trenches are planted, leave the superfluous earth in ridges between the rows till by the subsidence of the earth it becomes necessary to pull it into the trenches. if any of your grapes turn out illy, cut off the vine & ingraft another on the stock. an acre in vines where they are 2½ f apart in the row will admit 4316. in all.

IMPLEMENTS AND MACHINERY

Wherever Jefferson went, he was on the lookout for labor-saving implements and machinery that could be adapted to use on his farm and in the United States generally. He was among the first American users of the Scotch threshing machine, and he developed a hemp brake.

Most important, however, of his contributions in this field of activity was his moldboard for plows. It is mentioned in his records as early as April 1788, but it was not completed and made available until nearly a decade later. It attracted wide attention in scientific circles, especially in Europe, and led to his receiving honorary memberships in various societies.

Threshing Machines

. . . . My threshing machine has arrived at New York. Mr. Pinckney writes me word that the original from which this model is copied, threshes 150 bushels of wheat in 8 hours, with 6 horses and 5 men. It may be moved either by water or horses. Fortunately the workman who made it (a millwright) is come in the same vessel to settle in America. I have written to persuade him to go on immediately to Richmond, offering him the use of my model to exhibit, and to give him letters to get him into immediate employ in making them. I expect an answer before I write to you again. I understand that the model is made mostly in brass, and in the simple form in which it was first ordered, to be worked by horses. It was to have cost 5 guineas, but Mr. Pinckney having afterwards directed it to be accommodated to water movement also, it has made it more complicated, and costs 13 guineas. It will thresh any grain from the Windsor bean down to the smallest. Adieu.[24]

---

[24]Jefferson to James Madison, from Philadelphia, Sept. 1, 1793. For the complete letter, see Ford ed., 6:401-404; Lipscomb and Bergh ed., 9:211-215; and Washington ed., 4:52-54.

The Moldboard of Least Resistance

I have to acknowledge the receipt of your two favours of June 21, and July 15, and of several separate parcels containing the agricultural reports. These now form a great mass of information on a subject, of all in the world, the most interesting to man: for none but the husbandman makes any thing for him to eat; and he who can double his food, as your exertions bid fair to do, deserves to rank, among his benefactors, next after his Creator. Among so many reports of transcendent merit, one is unwilling to distinguish particulars. Yet the application of the new chemistry, to the subject of manures, the discussion of the question on the size of farms, the treatise on the potatoe, from their universality have an advantage in other countries over those which are topographical. The work which shall be formed, as the result of the whole, we shall expect with impatience.

Permit me, through you, to make here my acknowledgements to the board of agriculture for the honour they have been pleased to confer on me by, associating me to their institution. In love for the art, I am truly their associate: but events have controuled my predilection for its practice, and denied to me that uninterrupted attention, which alone can enable us to advance in it with a sure step. Perhaps I may find opportunities of being useful to you as a centinel at an outpost, by conveying intelligence of whatever may occur here new and interesting to agriculture. This duty I shall perform with pleasure, as well in respectful return for the notice of the board, as from a zeal for improving the condition of human life, by an interchange of its comforts, and of the information which may increase them. . . .

In a former letter to you I mentioned the construction of the mould-board of a plough which had occurred to me, as advantageous in its form, as certain and invariable in the method of obtaining it with precision. I remember that Mr. Strickland of York, a member of your board, was so well satisfied with the principles on which it was formed that he took some drawings of it; and some others have considered it with the same approbation. An experience of five years has enabled me to say, it answers in practice to what it promises in theory. The mould-board should be a continuation of the wing of the ploughshare, beginning at its hinder edge, and in the same plane. Its first office is to receive the sod horizontally from the wing, to raise it to a proper height for being turned over, and to make, in its progress, *the least resistance possible;* and consequently to require a minimum in the moving power. Were this its only office, the wedge would offer itself as the most* eligible form in practice. But the sod is to be turned over also. To do this, the one edge of it is not to be raised at all; for to raise this would be a waste of labour. The other edge is to be raised till it passes the perpendicular, that it may fall over with its own weight. And that this may be done so as to give also the least resistance, it must be made to rise gradually from the moment the sod is received. The mould-board then, in this second office, operates as a transverse, or rising wedge, the point of which sliding back horizontally on the ground, the other end continues rising till it passes the perpendicular. Or, to vary the point of view, place on the ground a wedge of the breadth of the ploughshare, of its length from the wing backwards, and as high at the heel as it is wide. Draw a diagonal

---

*I am aware that were the turf only *to be raised* to a given height in a given length of mould-board, and not to be turned over, the form of least resistance would not be rigorously a wedge with both faces straight, but with the upper one curved according to the laws of the solid of least resistance described by the mathematicians. But the difference between the effect of the curved and of the plain wedge, in the case of a mould-board, is so minute, and the difficulty in the execution which the former would superinduce on common workmen is so great, that the plain wedge is the most eligible to be assumed in practice for the first element of our construction.

on its upper face from the left angle at the point to the right upper angle of the heel. Bevil the fact from the diagonal to the right-bottom-edge which lies on the ground. That half is then evidently in the best form for performing the two offices of raising and turning the sod gradually, and with the least effort: and if you will suppose the same bevil continued across the left side of the diagonal, that is, if you will suppose a straight line whose length is at least equal to the breadth of the wedge, applied on the face of the first bevil and moved backwards on it parallel with itself and with the ends of the wedge, the lower end of the line moving along the right-bottom-edge, a curved plane will be generated, whose characteristic will be a combination of the principle of the wedge in cross directions, and will give what we seek, the *mould-board of least resistance*. It offers too this great advantage, that it may be made by the coarsest workman, by a process so exact that its form shall never be varied a single hair's breadth. One fault of all other mould-boards is that, being copied by the eye, no two will be alike. In truth it is easier to form the mould-board I speak of with precision, when the method has been once seen, than to describe that method either by words or figures. I will attempt however to describe it. Whatever may not be intelligible from the description may be supplied from the model I send you.

Let the breadth and depth of the furrow the farmer usually opens, as also the length of his plough-bar, from where it joins the wing to the hinder end, be given; as these fix the dimensions of the block of which the mould-board is to be made. Suppose the furrow 9 inches wide, 6 inches deep, and the plough-bar 2 feet long. Then the block, Fig. 1. must be 9 inches wide at bottom (b. c.) 13½ inches wide at top, (a. d.) because if it were merely of the same width with the bottom as a.e. the sod, only raised to the perpendicular, would fall back into the furrow by its own elasticity. I find from experience, that, in my soil, the top of the mould-board should overjet the perpendicular 4½ inches in a height of 12 inches, to insure that the weight of the sod shall preponderate over its elasticity. This is an angle of nearly 22°. The block must be 12 inches high, because, unless the mould-board be in height double the depth of the furrow, in ploughing friable earth, it will be thrown in waves over the mouldboard: and it must be 3 feet long, one foot of which is added to form a tail-piece, by which it may be made fast to the plough-handle. The first operation is to give the first form to this tail-piece, by sawing the block, Fig. 2. across from a. b. on its left side, (which is 12 inches from its hinder end) along the line b. c. to c. within 1½ inches of the right side, and to the corresponding point in the bottom, 1½ inches also from the side. Then saw in again at the hinder end from d. e. (1½ inches from the right side) along the line d. c. The block a. b. c. d. e. f. g. drops out and leaves the tail-piece c. d. e. h. i. k. 1½ inches thick. The fore part of the block a. b. c. k. l. m. n. is what is to form the real mould-board. With a carpenter's square make a scribe all round the block at every inch. There will of course be 23 of them. Then from the point k. Fig. 2. and 3. draw the diagonals k. m. on the top, and k. o. Fig. 3. on the right side. Enter a saw at the point m. being the left-fore-upper corner, and saw in, guiding the hinder part of the saw along the diagonal m. k. (Fig. 2. 3.) and the fore part down the left edge of the block at the fore-end m. l. (Fig. 2.) till it reaches k. and l. in a straight line. It will then have reached the true central diagonal of the block k. l. Fig. 5. then enter the saw at the point o. being the right-fore-bottom corner, and saw in, guiding the hinder part of the saw along the diagonal o. k. (Fig. 3.) and the fore part along the bottom edge of the fore end o. l. till it again reaches k. l. Fig. 5. the same central diagonal to which you had cut in the other direction. Consequently the pyramid k. m. n. o. l. Fig. 4. drops out and leaves the block in the form Fig. 5. You will now observe that if in the last operation, instead of stopping the saw at the central diagonal k. l. we had cut through the block in the same plane, we should have taken off a wedge *l. m. n. o. k. b.* Fig. 3. and left the block in the form of a wedge also *l. o. k. b. a. p. k.* which, when speaking of the principle of the mould-board, I observed would be the most perfect form if it had only to raise the sod. But as it is to be turned over also, the left half of the upper wedge is preserved, to furnish on the left side, the continuation of the bevil which was proposed to be made on the right half of the bottom wedge. We are now to proceed to the bevil, for which purpose the scribes round the block were formed before the pyramidal piece was taken out; and attention must be used not to mismatch or mistake them, now that they are disjoined by the withdrawing of that piece. Enter the saw on the two points of the 1st scribe where it has been disjoined, which is exactly where it intersected the two superficial diagonals, and saw across the hollow of the block, guiding the saw, both before and behind, along the same scribe, till the fore part of the saw reaches the bottom edge of the right side, and the middle of the saw reaches the central diagonal; the hinder part will of course continue the same straight line, which will issue somewhere on the top of the block. Then enter the saw in like manner on the two projecting points of the 2d scribe, and saw in, along the scribe, before and behind, till it reaches the same bottom edge of the right side, and the central diagonal. Then the 3d, 4th, 5th, &c. scribes successively. After cutting in several of the earlier scribes, the hinder part of the saw will issue at the left side of the block, and all the scribes being cut, the saw will have left straight lines from the bottom edge of the right side of the block, across the central diagonal. With an adze dub off all the sawed parts to the bottoms of the saw-marks, just leaving the traces visible, and the face of the mould-board is finished. These traces will shew how the cross wedge rises gradually on the face of the direct wedge, which is preserved in trace of the central diagonal. A person may represent to himself, sensibly and easily the manner in which the sod is raised on this mould-board, by describing on the ground a parallelogram 2 feet long and 9 inches broad, as *a. b. c. d.* Fig. 6 then rest one end of a stick 27½ inches long on the ground at *b.* and raise the other 12 inches high at *e.* which is 4½ inches from *d.* and represents the overhanging of that side of the mould-board. Then present another stick 12 inches long from *a.* to *b.* and move it backwards parallel with itself from *a. b.* to *d. c.* keeping one end of it always on the line *a. d.* and letting the other rise as it recedes along the diagonal stick *b. e.* which represents our central diagonal. The motion of the cross stick will be that of our rising wedge, and will shew how every transverse line of the sod is conducted from its first horizontal position, till it is raised so far beyond the perpendicular as to fall reversed by its own weight. But to return to our work. We have still to form the under side of the mould-board. Turn the block bottom up. Enter the saw on the 1st scribe, at what was the bottom edge of the left side, and cut in, guiding the instrument at both ends by the scribe, till it has approached within an inch, or any other distance according to the thickness you choose, of the face. Then cut in like manner all the other scribes, and with the adze dub out the sawed parts, and the mould-board is done. It is to be made fast to the plough by resting the toe in the hinder edge of the wing, which must be made double like a comb-case, to receive and protect the fore end of the mould-board. Then pass a screw through the mould-board and helve of the ploughshare where they touch each other, and two others through the tail-piece of the mould-board and right handle of the plough, and cut off so much of the tail-piece as projects behind the handle, diagonally, and the whole is done.

I have described this operation in its simplest mode, that it might be the more easily understood. But, in practice, I have found some other modifications of it advantageous. Thus, instead of first forming my block as *a. b. c. d.* Fig. 7. where

$a.$ $b.$ is 12 inches, and the angle at $b.$ a right one, I cut a wedge-like piece $b.$ $c.$ $e.$ off of the bottom through the whole length of the block, $b.$ $e.$ being equal to the thickness of the bar of the share (suppose 1½ inches) because the face of the wing declining from the top of the bar to the ground, were the block laid on the share, without an equivalent bevil at its bottom, the side $a.$ $b.$ would decline from the perpendicular, and $a.$ $d.$ from its horizontal position. Again, instead of leaving the top of the block 13½ inches wide from $m.$ to $n.$ Fig. 8. I cut a wedge from the right side $n.$ $k.$ $i.$ $c.$ $p.$ $m.$ 1½ inches thick at top and tapering to nothing at bottom; because I find that the tail-piece, being by this means made oblique, as $c.$ $i.$ instead of $k.$ $i.$ is brought more advantageously to the side of the handle. The first superficial diagonal is consequently brought from $m.$ to $c.$ and not from $m.$ to $k.$ as in the first directions. These variations will be easy to any one after understanding the general principle. While these mould-boards have been under trial, and essays have been making of greater or less projections for the upper right edge of the block, and of different heights in proportion to the depth of the furrow, I have continued to make them of wood. But now satisfied by a sufficient experience, that for a furrow of 9 by 6 inches, the dimensions I have stated are the best, I propose to have the mould-board made of cast iron.

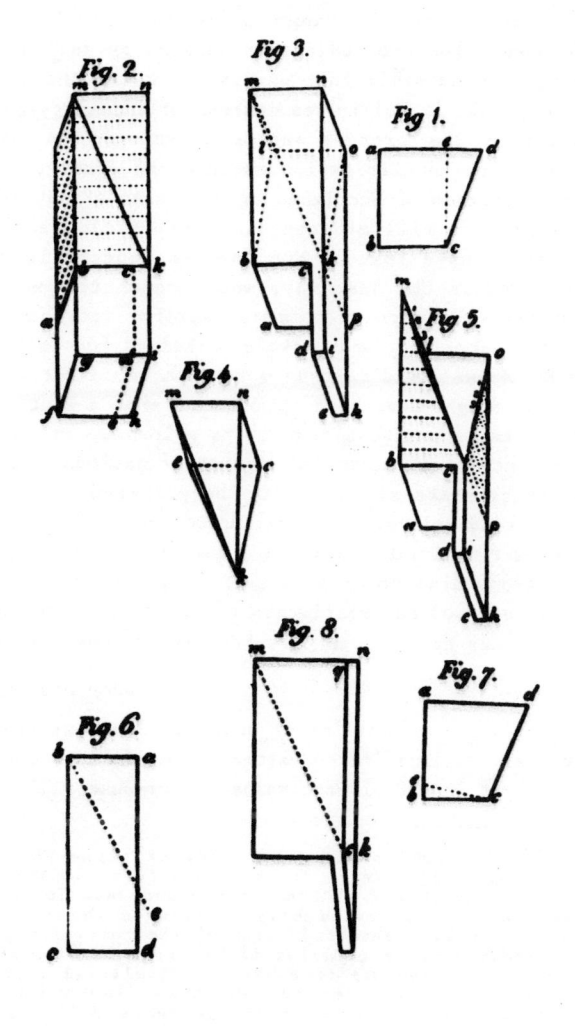

I am sensible that this description may be thought too lengthy and elaborate for a subject which has hardly been deemed worthy the application of science. But if the plough be in truth the most useful of the instruments known to man, its perfection cannot be an idle speculation. And in any case whatever, the combination of a *theory* which may satisfy the learned, with a *practice* intelligible to the most unlettered labourer, will be acceptable to the two most useful classes of society. Be this as it may, from the widow her mite only was expected. I have contributed according to my poverty; others will from their abundance. — None so much as yourself, who have been the animating principle of the institution from its first germ. When I contemplate the extensive good which the proceedings under your direction are calculated to produce, I cannot but deplore every possibility of their interruption. I am fixed in awe at the mighty conflict to which two great nations are advancing, and recoil with horror at the ferociousness of man. Will nations never devise a more rational umpire of differences than force? Are there no means of coercing injustice more gratifying to our nature than a waste of the blood of thousands, and of the labour of millions of our fellow-creatures? We see numerous societies of men (the aboriginals of this country) living together without the acknowledgment of either laws or magistracy. Yet they live in peace among themselves, and acts of violence and injury are as rare in their societies as in nations which keep the sword of the law in perpetual activity. Public reproach, a refusal of common offices, interdiction of the commerce and comforts of society are found as effectual as the coarser instrument of force. Nations, like these individuals, stand towards each other only in the relations of natural right. Might they not, like them, be peaceably punished for violence and wrong? Wonderful has been the progress of human improvement in other lines. Let us hope then that that law of nature which makes a virtuous conduct produce benefit, and vice loss, to the agent in the long run, which has sanctioned the common principle that honesty is the best policy, will in time influence the proceedings of nations as well as of individuals; and that we shall at length be sensible that war is an instrument entirely inefficient towards redressing wrong; that it multiplies instead of indemnifying losses. Had the money which has been spent in the present war been employed in making roads and conducting canals of navigation and irrigation through the country, not a hovel in the remotest corner of the Highlands of Scotland, or mountains of Auvergne, would have been without a boat at its door, a rill of water in every field, and a road to its market town. Had the money we have lost by the lawless depredations of all the belligerent powers been employed in the same way, what communications would have been opened of roads and waters! Yet were we to go to war for redress, instead of redress, we should plunge deeper into loss, and disable ourselves for half a century more from attaining the same end. A war would cost us more than would cut through the isthmus of Darien; and that of Suez might have been opened with what a single year has seen thrown away on the rock of Gibraltar. These truths are palpable, and must in the progress of time have their influence on the minds and conduct of nations. An evidence that we are advancing towards a better state of things may be gathered from the public patronage of your labours, which tend eminently to ameliorate the condition of man. That they may meet the success they merit, I sincerely pray, and that yourself may receive the patriot's best reward, the applauding voice of present and future times. Accept, I beseech you, mine, with assurances of the sentiments of great and sincere respect and esteem with which I have the honour to be, Dear Sir, Your affectionate friend, and humble servant.[25]

Hemp Brakes

.... Your letter being evidence of your attention to mechanical things, and to their application to matters of daily interest, I will mention a trifle in this way, which yet is not without value. I presume, like the rest of us in the country, you are

---

[25] Jefferson to Sir John Sinclair, from Philadelphia, Mar. 23, 1798, in American Philosophical Society, *Transactions* (o.s.) 4:313-322 (1799).
The moldboard of least resistance was Jefferson's most important agricultural invention. It has an important place in the several decades of research and invention that preceded the introduction of the cast-iron plow by Jethro Wood in 1814. It demonstrated the value of using mathematics in plow construction and thus removed guesswork from the manufacture of a basic agricultural implement. The persistence of Jefferson's interest also influenced subsequent invention appreciably. See Lewis Cecil Gray, *History of Agriculture in the Southern United States to 1860*, 2:792-800 (Washington, 1933); and Leo Rogin, *The Introduction of Farm Machinery in its Relation to the Agriculture of the United States during the Nineteenth Century*, 3-31 (Berkeley, 1931).

in the habit of household manufacture, and that you will not, like too many, abandon it on the return of peace, to enrich our late enemy, and to nourish foreign agents in our bosom, whose baneful influence and intrigues cost us so much embarrassment and dissension. The shirting for our laborers has been an object of some difficulty. Flax is injurious to our lands, and of so scanty produce that I have never attempted it. Hemp, on the other hand, is abundantly productive, and will grow forever on the same spot. But the breaking and beating it, which has been always done by hand, is so slow, so laborious, and so much complained of by our laborers, that I had given it up and purchased and manufactured cotton for their shirting. The advanced price of this, however, now makes it a serious item of expense; and in the meantime, a method of removing the difficulty of preparing hemp occurred to me, so simple and so cheap, that I return to its culture and manufacture. To a person having a threshing machine, the addition of a hemp-break will not cost more than twelve or fifteen dollars. You know that the first mover in that machine is a horizontal horse-wheel with cogs on its upper face. On these is placed a wallower and shaft, which give motion to the threshing apparatus. On the opposite side of this same wheel I place another wallower and shaft, through which, and near its outer end, I pass a cross-arm of sufficient strength, projecting on each side fifteen inches in this form: nearly under the cross-arm is placed a very strong hemp-break, much stronger and heavier than those for the hand. Its head block particularly is massive, and four feet high, and near its upper end, in front, is fixed a strong pin (which we may call its horn); by this the cross-arm lifts and lets fall the break twice in every revolution of the wallower. A man feeds the break with hemp stalks, and a little person holds under the head block a large twist of the hemp which has been broken, resembling a twist of tobacco but larger, where it is more perfectly beaten than I have ever seen done by hand. If the horse-wheel has one hundred and forty-four cogs, the wallower eleven rounds, and the horse goes three times round in a minute, it will give about eighty strokes in a minute. I had fixed a break to be moved by the gate of my saw-mill, which broke and beat at the rate of two hundred pounds a day. But the inconveniences of interrupting that, induced me to try the power of a horse, and I have found it to answer perfectly. The power being less, so also probably will be the effect, of which I cannot make a fair trial until I commence on my new crop. I expect that a single horse will do the breaking and beating of ten men. Something of this kind has been so long wanted by the cultivators of hemp, that as soon as I can speak of its effect with certainty, I shall probably describe it anonymously in the public papers, in order to forestall the prevention of its use by some interloping patentee. I shall be happy to learn that an actual experiment of your steam engine fulfils the expectations we form of it, and I pray you to accept the assurances of my esteem and respect.[26]

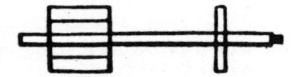

ROTATIONS

The lands at Monticello suffered from neglect under overseers during Jefferson's long absences in the public service. To restore them to productivity, Jefferson worked out a system of crop rotation which is described in the following letter.

. . . . I find on a more minute examination of my lands than the short visits heretofore made to them permitted, that a ten years' abandonment of them to the ravages of overseers, has brought on them a degree of degradation far beyond what I had expected.

As this obliges me to adopt a milder course of cropping, so I find that they have enabled me to do it, by having opened a great deal of lands during my absence. I have therefore determined on a division of my farm into six fields, to be put under this rotation: first year, wheat; second, corn, potatoes, peas; third, rye or wheat, according to circumstances; fourth and fifth, clover where the fields will bring it, and buckwheat dressings where they will not; sixth, folding, and buckwheat dressings. But it will take me from three to six years to get this plan underway. I am not yet satisfied that my acquisition of overseers from the head of Elk has been a happy one, or that much will be done this year towards rescuing my plantations from their wretched condition. Time, patience and perserverance must be the remedy; and the maxim of your letter, "slow and sure," is not less a good one in agriculture than in politics. . . . With every wish for your health and happiness, and my most friendly respects for Mrs. Washington, I have the honor to be, dear Sir, your most obedient, and most humble servant.[27]

EROSION CONTROL

Horizontal plowing as a method of erosion control was practiced by Jefferson and his son-in-law, Thomas Mann Randolph. The following descriptions are, therefore, of special interest.

. . . . The present delightful weather has drawn us all into our farms and gardens; we have had the most devastating rain which has ever fallen within my knowledge. Three inches of water fell in the space of about an hour. Every hollow of every hill presented a torrent which swept everything before it. I have never seen the fields so much injured. Mr. Randolph's farm [Edgehill] is the only one which has not suffered; his horizontal furrows arrested the water at every step till it was absorbed, or at least had deposited the soil it had taken up. Everybody in this neighborhood is adopting his method of ploughing, except tenants who have no interest in the preservation of the soil. . . .[28]

. . . . A method of ploughing over hill sides horizontally, introduced into the most hilly part of our country by Colo. T. M. Randolph, my son in law, may be worth mentioning to you. He has practiced it a dozen or 15 years, and it's advantages were so immediately observed that it has already become very general, and has entirely changed and renovated the face of our country. Every rain, before that, while it gave a temporary refreshment, did permanent evil by carrying off our soil: and fields were no sooner cleared than wasted. At present we may say that we lose none of our soil, the rain not absorbed in the moment of it's fall being retained in the hollows between the beds until it can be absorbed. Our practice is when we first enter on this process, with a rafter level of 10 f. span, to lay off guide lines conducted horizontally around the hill or valley from one end to the other of the field, and about 30 yards apart. The steps of the level on the ground are marked by a stroke of a hoe, and immediately

---

[27] Jefferson to President Washington, from Monticello, May 14, 1794. For the complete letter, see Ford ed., 6:509-510; Lipscomb and Bergh ed., 9:286-288; and Washington ed., 4:105-107.
[28] Jefferson to William A. Burwell, from Monticello, Feb. 25, 1810. For the complete letter, see Lipscomb and Bergh ed., 12:363-365; and Washington ed., 5:504-506. For a scholarly discussion of horizontal plowing in ante-bellum Virginia, see A. R. Hall, "Early Erosion-Control Practices in Virginia," U. S. Department o. Agriculture, *Miscellaneous Publication 256*, p. 15-20 (Washington, D. C., 1937).

followed by a plough to preserve the trace. A man or a lad, with a level, and two small boys, the one with sticks, the other with the hoe, will do an acre of this in an hour, and when once done it is forever done. We generally level a field the year it is put into Indian corn laying it into beds of 6 ft. wide, with a large water furrow between the beds, until all the fields have been once leveled. The intermediate furrows are run by the eye of the ploughman governed by these guide lines, & occasion gores which are thrown into short beds. As in ploughing very steep hill sides horizontally the common ploughman can scarcely throw the furrow up hill, Colo. Randolph has contrived a very simple alteration of the share, which throws the furrow down hill both going and coming. It is as if two shares were welded together at their straight side and at a right angle with each other. This turns on it's bar as on a pivot, so as to lay either share horizontal, when the other becoming verticle acts as a mould board. This is done by the ploughman in an instant by a single motion of the hand, at the end of every furrow. . . . Horizontal and deep ploughing, with the use of plaister and clover, which are but beginning to be used here will, as we believe, restore this part of our country to it's original fertility, which was exceeded by no upland in the state. . . .[29]

CROPS

Jefferson's curiosity about new crops was apparently never satisfied. He tried out an almost countless number in his gardens and fields. He was, however, especially interested in clover and legumes as soil-restoring crops. The following letters provide reports on his experiences with these and other crops.

Red Clover

. . . . My little essay in red clover, the last year, has had the most encouraging success. I sowed then about forty acres. I have sowed this year about one hundred and twenty, which the rain now falling comes very opportunely on. From one hundred and sixty to two hundred acres, will be my yearly sowing. The seed-box described in the agricultural transactions of New York, reduces the expense of seeding from six shillings to two shillings and three pence the acre, and does the business better than is possible to be done by the human hand. May we hope a visit from you? If we may, let it be after the middle of May, by which time I hope to be returned from Bedford. . . .[30]

Peas and Clover

. . . . I . . . talk to you of my peas and clover. As to the latter article, I have great encouragement from the friendly nature of our soil. I think I have had, both the last and present year, as good clover from common grounds, which had brought several crops of wheat and corn without ever having been manured, as I ever saw on the lots around Philadelphia. I verily believe that a yield of thirty-four acres, sowed on wheat April was twelvemonth, has given me a ton to the acre at its first cutting this spring. The stalks extended, measured three and a half feet long very commonly.

---

[29] Jefferson to Tristam Dalton, from Monticello, May 2, 1817, in Ford ed., 10:79-80.

[30] Jefferson to James Madison, from Monticello Apr. 27, 1795. For the complete letter, see Ford ed., 7:8-11; Lipscomb and Bergh ed., 9:301-304; and Washington ed., 4:116-118.

Another field, a year older, and which yielded as well the last year, has sensibly fallen off this year. My exhausted fields bring a clover not high enough for hay, but I hope to make seed from it. Such as these, however, I shall hereafter put into peas in the broadcast, proposing that one of my sowings of wheat shall be after two years of clover, and the other after two years of peas. I am trying the white boiling pea of Europe (the Albany pea) this year, till I can get the hog pea of England, which is the most productive of all. But the true winter vetch is what we want extremely. I have tried this year the Carolina drill. It is absolutely perfect. Nothing can be more simple, nor perform its office more perfectly for a single row. I shall try to make one to sow four rows at a time of wheat or peas, at twelve inches distance. I have one of the Scotch threshing machines nearly finished. It is copied exactly from a model Mr. Pinckney sent me, only that I have put the whole works (except the horse wheel) into a single frame, movable from one field to another on the two axles of a wagon. It will be ready in time for the harvest which is coming on, which will give it a full trial. Our wheat and rye are generally fine, and the prices talked of bid fair to indemnify us for the poor crops of the last two years. . . . [31]

Other Introductions

I have to acknowledge the receipt of your favors of August 16th and 18th, together with the box of seed accompanying the former, which has just come to hand. The letter of the 4th of June, which you mention to have committed to Mr. King, has never been received. It has most likely been intercepted on the sea, now become a field of lawless and indiscriminate rapine and violence. The first box which came through Mr. Donald, arrived safely the last year, but being a little too late for that season, its contents have been divided between Mr. Randolph and myself, and will be committed to the earth now immediately. The peas and the vetch are most acceptable indeed. Since you were here, I have tried that species of your field pea which is cultivated in New York, and begin to fear that that plant will scarcely bear our sun and soil. A late acquisition too of a species of our country pea, called the cow pea, has pretty well supplied the place in my husbandry which I had destined for the European field pea. It is very productive, excellent food for man and beast, awaits without loss our leisure for gathering, and shades the ground very closely through the hottest months of the year. This with the loosening of the soil, I take to be the chief means by which the pea improves the soil. We know that the sun in our cloudless climate is the most powerful destroyer of fertility in naked ground, and therefore that the perpetual fallows will not do here, which are so beneficial in a cloudy climate. Still I shall with care try all the several kinds of pea you have been so good as to send me, and having tried all hold fast that which is good. Mr. Randolph is peculiarly happy in having the barleys committed to him, as he had been desirous of going considerably into that culture. I was able at the same time to put into his hands Siberian barley, sent me from France. I look forward with considerable anxiety to the success of the winter vetch, for it gives us a good winter crop, and helps the succeeding summer one. It is something like doubling the produce of the field. I know it does well in Italy, and therefore have the more hope here. My experience leaves me no fear as to the success of clover. I have never seen finer than in some of my fields which have never been manured. My rotation is triennial; to wit, one year of wheat and two of

---

[31] Jefferson to President Washington, from Monticello, June 19, 1796. For the complete letter, see Ford ed., 7:81-85; Lipscomb and Bergh ed., 9:339-343; and Washington ed., 4:141-144.

clover in the stronger fields, or two of peas in the weaker, with a crop of Indian corn and potatoes between every other rotation, that is to say once in seven years. Under this easy course of culture, aided with some manure, I hope my fields will recover their pristine fertility, which had in some of them been completely exhausted by perpetual crops of Indian corn and wheat alternately. The atmosphere is certainly the great workshop of nature for elaborating the fertilizing principles and insinuating them into the soil. It has been relied on as the sole means of regenerating our soil by most of the land-holders in the canton I inhabit, and where rest has been resorted to before a total exhaustion, the soil has never failed to recover. If, indeed, it be so run down as to be incapable of throwing weeds or herbage of any kind, to shade the soil from the sun, it either goes off in gullies, and is entirely lost, or remains exhausted till a growth springs up of such trees as will rise in the poorest soils. Under the shade of these and the cover soon formed of their deciduous leaves, and a commencing herbage, such fields sometimes recover in a long course of years; but this is too long to be taken into a course of husbandry. Not so, however, is the term within which the atmosphere alone will reintegrate a soil rested in due season. A year of wheat will be balanced by one, two or three years of rest and atmospheric influence, according to the quality of the soil. It has been said that no rotation of crops will keep the earth in the same degree of fertility without the aid of manure. But it is well known here that a space of rest greater or less in spontaneous herbage, will restore the exhaustion of a single crop. This then is a rotation; and as it is not to be believed that spontaneous herbage is the only or best covering during rest, so may we expect that a substitute for it may be found which will yield profitable crops. Such perhaps are clover, peas, vetches, &c. A rotation then may be found, which by giving time for the slow influence of the atmosphere, will keep the soil in a constant and equal state of fertility. But the advantage of manuring, is that it will do more in one than the atmosphere would require several years to do, and consequently enables you so much the oftener to take exhausting crops from the soil, a circumstance of importance where there is more labor than land. I am much indebted.[32]

LIVESTOCK

Improving American livestock was still another of Jefferson's interests, and the following letters are selected to illustrate this phase of his farming activities. The plan for distributing Merino rams throughout Virginia which is outlined in the letter to Madison may be considered a precursor of the cooperative breeding circuits or clubs of recent years.

Merino Sheep

I thank you for your promised attention to my portion of the Merinos, and if there be any expenses of transportation, &c., and you will be so good as to advance my portion of them with yours and notify the amount, it shall be promptly remitted. What shall we do with them? I have been so disgusted with the scandalous extortions lately practised in the sale of these animals, and with the description of patriotism and praise to the sellers, as if the thousands of dollars apiece they have not been ashamed to receive were not reward enough, that I am disposed to consider as right, whatever is the reverse of what they have done. Since fortune has put the occasion upon us, is it

---

[32] Jefferson to _____, from Philadelphia, Mar. 23, 1798, in Lipscomb and Bergh ed., 10: 11-14; and Washington ed., 4: 223-225.

not incumbent upon us so to dispense this benefit to the farmers of our country, as to put to shame those who, forgetting their own wealth and the honest simplicity of the farmers, have thought them fit objects of the shaving art, and to excite, by a better example, the condemnation due to theirs? No sentiment is more acknowledged in the family of Agriculturists, than that the few who can afford it should incur the risk and expense of all new improvements, and give the benefit freely to the many of more restricted circumstances. The question then recurs, What are we to do with them? I shall be willing to concur with you in any plan you shall approve, and in order that we may have some proposition to begin upon, I will throw out a first idea, to be modified or postponed to whatever you shall think better.

Give all the full-blooded males we can raise to the different counties of our State, one to each, as fast as we can furnish them. And as there must be some rule of priority for the distribution, let us begin with our own counties, which are contiguous and nearly central to the State, and proceed, circle after circle, till we have given a ram to every county. This will take about seven years, if we add to the full descendants those which will have past to the fourth generation from common ewes. To make the benefit of a single male as general as practicable to the county, we may ask some known character in each county to have a small society formed which shall receive the animal and prescribe rules for his care and government. We should retain ourselves all the full-blooded ewes, that they may enable us the sooner to furnish a male to every county. When all shall have been provided with rams, we may, in a year or two more, be in a condition to give an ewe also to every county, if it be thought necessary. But I suppose it will not, as four generations from their full-blooded ram will give them the pure race from common ewes.

In the meantime we shall not be without a profit indemnifying our trouble and expense. For if of our present stock of common ewes, we place with the ram as many as he may be competent to, suppose fifty, we may sell the male lambs of every year for such reasonable price as, in addition to the wool, will pay for the maintenance of the flock. The first year they will be half-bloods, the second three-quarters, the third seven-eights, and the fourth full-blooded; if we take care in selling annually half the ewes also, to keep those of highest blood, this will be a fund for kindnesses to our friends, as well as for indemnification to ourselves; and our whole State may thus, from this small stock, so dispersed, be filled in a very few years with this valuable race, and more satisfaction result to ourselves than money ever administered to the bosom of a shaver. . . .[33]

Shepherd Dogs

Your information is correct that we possess here the genuine race of Shepherd dogs. I imported them from France about 4 years ago. They were selected for me by the Marquis Fayette, and I have endeavored to secure their preservation by giving them, always in pairs, to those who wished them. I have a pair myself at different places; where I suffer no other dog to be; and there are others in the neighborhood. I have no doubt therefore that from some of these we can furnish a pair, or perhaps two, at any time when Judge Todd can send for them; he giving me some notice to seek out a litter in a proper state for traveling. There are so many applications for them that there

---

[33] Jefferson to President Madison, from Monticello, May 13, 1810, in Lipscomb and Bergh ed., 12:389-391; and Washington ed., 5:522-524.

are never any on hand, unless kept on purpose. Their extraordinary sagacity renders them extremely valuable, capable of being taught almost any duty that may be required of them, and the most anxious in the performance of that duty, the most watchful and faithful of all servants. But they must be reasonably fed; and are the better for being attached to a master. If they are forced by neglect and hunger to prowl for themselves, their sagacity renders them the most destructive marauders imaginable. You will see your flock of sheep and of hogs disappearing from day to day, without ever being able to detect them in it. They learn readily to go for the cows of an evening, or for the sheep, to drive up the chickens, ducks, turkies every one into their own house, to keep forbidden animals from the yard, all of themselves and at the proper hour, and are the most watchful housedogs in the world. I shall be happy in an occasion of being useful to you by putting you in stock with them, and avail myself of this occasion of renewing to you the assurance of my high esteem and respect.[34]

HOUSEHOLD MANUFACTURES

When Jefferson began to develop his home at Monticello, the transfer of manufactures from households to factories had barely begun, and self-sufficiency was a necessity as well as an objective for every farm. In addition, however, Jefferson established a nailery with a view to supplementing his cash income. The first letter that follows relates to this undertaking.

The letter to Adams is interesting not only for its account of the household manufactures at Monticello but because it marked the renewal of the close friendship of the two men. Due to the political controversies of the 1790s, they had become estranged. From this time till their deaths on the same day, July 4, 1826, they corresponded regularly.

The Nailery

. . . . I take the liberty of enclosing some nail cards, which I will thank you to put into the hands of such of your merchants as you think substantial and punctual. Mr. Stuart, Mr. Sinclair, Gamble & _____, have been named to me as such, and probably others. I deliver the nails at Charlottesville or Milton at the *wholesale* Richmond price at the time-being. This is certified to me monthly by Mr. Robert Pollard, of Richmond. Payment is expected in 3 months after they go out of my hands. I am now executing an order for Dr. Johnson of your town, which will give them a sample of my nails. Our harvest, commencing now within a few days, will suspend our work probably a month from this time. Any orders may be executed after that time at the rate of about 80 lbs. a day. I sell by the pound altogether, and the merchants here retail by the pound at about 25 per cent. on my prices. My barrels contain from about 125 to 175 lbs., according to the size of the nail. I note the present prices below.[35]

Weaving

I thank you before hand (for they are not yet arrived) for the specimens of homespun you have been so kind as to forward me by post. I doubt not their excellence, knowing how far you are advanced in these things in your quarter. Here we do little in

---

[34] Jefferson to Henry Innis, from Monticello, Sept. 18, 1813, in Coolidge Collection, Massachusetts Historical Society. The letter is here printed with the permission of the Society.

[35] Jefferson to Archibald Stuart, from Monticello, June 11, 1795, in *William and Mary College Quarterly Historical Magazine* (ser. 2), 5:293-294 (1925).

the fine way, but in course and middling goods a great deal. Every family in the country is a manufactory within itself; and is very generally able to make within itself all the stouter and middling stuffs for its own clothing and household use. We consider a sheep for every person in the family as sufficient to clothe it, in addition to the cotton, hemp and flax which we raise ourselves. For fine stuff we shall depend on your northern manufactories. Of these, that is to say, of company establishments, we have none. We use little machinery. The spinning jenny, and loom with the flying shuttle, can be managed in a family; but nothing more complicated. The economy and thriftiness resulting from our household manufactures are such that they will never again be laid aside; and nothing more salutary for us has ever happened than the British obstructions to our demands for their manufactures. Restore free intercourse when they will, their commerce with us will have totally changed its form, and the articles we shall in future want from them will not exceed their own consumption of our produce. . . .[36]

SHARING WITH OTHERS

Jefferson was invariably generous and thoughtful in sharing his agricultural discoveries with friends and acquaintances. As indicated in the following letters, he not only distributed seeds and plants from Monticello to be tried out in other communities but supplied careful instructions on their culture and use. As his insatiable interest in new crops gradually became known, many individuals sent him rare and unusual seeds and his farm became a veritable clearing house and distribution center.

Millet

Overhauling my seeds reminded me that I was to send you some Millet seed. It is now inclosed. Put it into drills 3 or 4 feet apart so that you may conveniently plough it, and the stalks at 6 inches distance in the drill. It is planted immediately after corn planting, say in May. It is to be used for the table as hominy, boiled or fried, needs neither husking nor beating, & boils in about two hours. It is believed here it will yield 100 bushels to the acre. I shall have some acres of it this year. Always affectionately yours.[37]

Strawberries

I promised to stock you with the Alpine strawberry as soon as my beds would permit. I now send you a basket of plants and can spare you 10 baskets more if you desire it. Their value, you know, is the giving strawberries 8 months in the year. But they require a large piece of ground and therefore I am moving them into the truck patch, as I cannot afford them room enough in the garden. I have received from McMahon some plants of the true Hudson strawberry. The last rains have brought them forwarded and ensured their living. I have been 20 years trying unsuccessfully to get them here. The next year I shall be able to stock you. I have received also from McMahon 4 plants

---

[36] Jefferson to John Adams, from Monticello, Jan. 21, 1812, in Ford ed., 9:332-334; Lipscomb and Bergh ed., 13:122-125; and Washington ed., 6:35-37. See also note 2, p. 6. For an account of Jefferson and Adams in retirement, see J. G. de Roulhac Hamilton, "Ripened Years: 1, John Adams Bold though Serene to the End; 2, Thomas Jefferson, Time Treated Him Kindly," *Century Magazine*, 114:281-291, 476-485 (1927).

[37] Jefferson to Fulwar Skipwith, from Monticello, Apr. 17, 1810, in the U. S. Department of Agriculture.

of his wonderful gooseberry. I measured the fruit of them 3 inches round. By the next year I hope they will afford you cuttings. About 20 plants of the Sprout kale have given us sprouts from the 1st of December. Their second growth now furnishes us a dish nearly every day, and they will enable me this year to stock my neighbors with the seed. We have now got the famous Irish grass, Fiorin, ensured and growing. They make hay from it in December, January, February. I received the plants from Ireland about a month ago. I am now engaged in planting a collection of pears. I know you have several kinds of very fine. If your nursery can spare 2 of each kind I will thank you for them: if not then some cuttings for engrafting, tying up each separately. Affectionately yours.[38]

Persian Melons

Th: Jefferson presents his salutations and respects to Mr White with his thanks for the Persian melonseed he has been so kind as to send him. He will endeavor to do it justice by his attentions, and especially to disperse it among his most careful acquaintances. It is by multiplying the good things of life that the mass of human happiness is increased, and the greatest of consolations to have contributed to it.[39]

Succory

Your favor of the 6th did not get to hand till the 23d and I now with pleasure send you as much of the succory seed as can well go under the volume of a letter. As I mentioned to our colleagues at the Gap, I had forgotten which of them expressed a willingness to try this plant, and therefore I have waited for their application having taken care to have a plenty of seed saved.

Sow the seed in rich beds, as you would tobacco seed, and take the advantage of good seasons in the spring to draw & transplant them. The ground should be well prepared by the plough. I have generally set the plants 18 inches or 2 feet apart every way, to give room for several weedings the 1st summer, for during that they are too weak to contend with the weeds. After that they will not be in danger from weeds. Do not cut the plants the 1st year that they may shed their seed and fill up all the intervals. The grazing of sheep destroys the plant. It is perennial, & of immense produce, and is a tolerable salad for the table in the spring, somewhat like the turnip tops but earlier. The warm spring bath proved extremely injurious to my health. I have been very poorly ever since, but within a week past have got on horseback, altho' not yet entirely well. Accept my friendly salutations & assurances of great esteem and respect.[40]

---

[38] Jefferson to George Divers, from Monticello, Mar. 10, 1812, in the Coolidge Collection, Massachusetts Historical Society. The letter is here printed with the permission of the Society.

[39] Jefferson to John Campbell White, from Monticello, Aug. 24, 1816, in the U. S. Department of Agriculture. Two of White's sons had secured the melon seed from Sir John Sinclair while traveling in England. The seed had been brought from Persia by Sir Gore Ouseley, the diplomat and oriental scholar. See White to Jefferson, from Baltimore, Aug. 13, 1816, in the U. S. Department of Agriculture.

[40] Jefferson to Henry C. Watkins, from Monticello, Nov. 27, 1818, in the U. S. Department of Agriculture.

JEFFERSON AND THE ADVANCEMENT OF AGRICULTURE

DEMOCRATIZATION OF LAND HOLDING

Having completed the drafting of the Declaration of Independence, Jefferson returned to Virginia to help forward a broad program of social reform.[41] He adhered passionately to the democratic philosophy that he had delineated in the Declaration and was resolved to eradicate every form of aristocracy, not only for his time but the future as well.

One phase of Jefferson's program was the abolition of entails and primogeniture which were the economic bases of landed estates. He wished to break up these large holdings and effect a wider distribution of property. Jefferson's own account of his efforts in this direction in the legislature of Virginia follows.

On the 12th of October, 1776, I obtained leave to bring in a bill declaring tenants in tail to hold their lands in fee simple. In the earlier times of the colony, when lands were to be obtained for little or nothing, some provident individuals procured large grants; and, desirous of founding great families for themselves, settled them on their descendants in fee tail. The transmission of this property from generation to generation, in the same name, raised up a distinct set of families, who, being privileged by law in the perpetuation of their wealth, were thus formed into a Patrician order, distinguished by the splendor and luxury of their establishments. From this order, too, the king habitually selected his counsellors of State; the hope of which distinction devoted the whole corps to the interests and will of the crown. To annul this privilege, and instead of an aristocracy of wealth, of more harm and danger, than benefit, to society, to make an opening for the aristocracy of virtue and talent, which nature has wisely provided for the direction of the interests of society, and scattered with equal hand through all its conditions, was deemed essential to a well-ordered republic. To effect it, no violence was necessary, no deprivation of natural right, but rather an enlargement of it by a repeal of the law. For this would authorize the present holder to divide the property among his children equally, as his affections were divided; and would place them, by natural generation, on the level of their fellow citizens. . . .

As the law of Descents, and the criminal law fell of course within my portion, I wished the committee to settle the leading principles of these, as a guide for me in framing them. . . . Mr. [Edmund] Pendleton wished to preserve the right of primogeniture, but seeing at once that that could not prevail, he proposed we should adopt the Hebrew principle, and give a double portion to the elder son. I observed, that if the eldest son could eat twice as much or do double work, it might be a natural evidence of his right to a double portion; but being on a par in his powers and wants, with his brothers and sisters, he should be on a par also in the partition of the patrimony; and such was the decision of the other members.[42]

---

[41] See J. Franklin Jameson, *The American Revolution Considered as a Social Movement* (Princeton, N. J., 1926).

[42] Jefferson's *Autobiography*, in Ford ed., 1:49-50, 59-60; Lipscomb and Bergh ed., 1:53-54, 64; and Washington ed., 1:36, 37, 43.

SETTLEMENT OF THE PUBLIC DOMAIN

As indicated in the introductory note to this compilation, Jefferson contributed materially to the formulation of the democratic principles covering the disposition of the public domain. The following letter provides a summary of the terms of land acquisition at the beginning of the nineteenth century and indicates Jefferson's ideas on European immigrants for the west.

Your favor of August 12th was yesterday received at this place, and I learn from it with pleasure that you have found a tract of country which will suit you for settlement. To us your first purchase would have been more gratifying, by adding yourself and your friends to our society; but the overruling consideration, with us as with you, is your own advantage, and as it would doubtless be a great comfort to you to have your ancient neighbors and friends settled around you. I sincerely wish that your proposition to "purchase a tract of land in the Illinois on favorable terms, for introducing a colony of English farmers," may encounter no difficulties from the established rules of our land department. The general law prescribes an open sale, where all citizens may compete an an equal footing for any lot of land which attracts their choice. To dispense with this in any particular case, requires a special law of Congress, and to special legislation we are generally averse, lest a principle of favoritism should creep in and pervert that of equal rights. It has, however, been done on some occasions where a special national advantage has been expected to overweight that of adherence to the general rule. The promised introduction of the culture of the vine procured a special law in favor of the Swiss settlement on the Ohio. That of the culture of oil, wine and other southern productions, did the same lately for the French settlement on the Tombigbee. It remains to be tried whether that of an improved system of farming, interesting to so great a proportion of our citizens, may not also be thought worth a dispensation with the general rule. This I suppose is the principal ground on which your proposition will be questioned. For although as to other foreigners it is thought better to discourage their settling together in large masses, wherein, as in our German settlements, they preserve for a long time their own languages, habits, and principles of government, and that they should distribute themselves sparsely among the natives for quicker amalgamation, yet English emigrants are without this inconvenience. They differ from us little but in their principles of government, and most of those (merchants excepted) who come here, are sufficiently disposed to adopt ours. What the issue, however, of your proposition may probably be, I am less able to advise you than many others; for during the last eight or ten years I have no knowledge of the administration of the land office or the principles of its government. Even the persons on whom it will depend are all changed within that interval, so as to leave me small means of being useful to you. Whatever they may be, however, they shall be freely exercised for your advantage, and that, not on the selfish principle of increasing our own population at the expense of other nations, for the additions to that from emigration are but as a drop in a bucket to those by natural procreation, but to consecrate a sanctuary for those whom the misrule of Europe may compel to seek happiness in other climes. This refuge once known will produce reaction on the happiness even of those who remain there, by warning their task-masters that when the evils of Egyptian oppression become heavier than those of the abandonment of country, another Canaan is open where their subjects will be received as brothers, and secured against like oppressions by a participation in the right of self-government. If additional motives could be wanting with us to the maintenance of this right, they would be found in the animating consideration that a single good government becomes thus a blessing to the whole earth, its welcome to the oppressed restraining within certain limits the measure of their oppressions. But should even this be counteracted by violence on the right of expatriation, the other branch of our example then presents itself for imitation, to rise on their rulers and do as we have done. You have set to your own country a good example, by showing them a peaceable mode of reducing their rulers to the necessity of becoming more wise, more moderate, and more honest, and I sincerely pray that the example may work for the benefit of those who cannot follow it, as it will for your own.

With Mr. Burckbeck, the associate of your late explanatory journeying, I have not the happiness of personal acquaintance; but I know him through his narrative of your journeyings together through France. The impressions received from that, give me confidence that a participation with yourself in assurances of the esteem and respect of a stranger will not be unacceptable to him, and the less when given through you and associated with those to yourself.[43]

INDIAN POLICY

Jefferson's sympathy for the original inhabitants of the United States dated from his youth. Although confronted with facts and not a theory, he sought to outline and strengthen a benevolent policy which looked toward their becoming settled farmers.

. . . . Although you will receive, through the official channel of the War Office, every communication necessary to develop to you our views respecting the Indians, and to direct your conduct, yet, supposing it will be satisfactory to you, and to those with whom you are placed, to understand my personal dispositions and opinions in this particular, I shall avail myself of this private letter to state them generally. I consider the business of hunting as already become insufficient to furnish clothing and subsistence to the Indians. The promotion of agriculture, therefore, and household manufacture, are essential in their preservation, and I am disposed to aid and encourage it liberally. This will enable them to live on much smaller portions of land, and, indeed, will render their vast forests useless but for the range of cattle; for which purpose, also, as they become better farmers, they will be found useless, and even disadvantageous. While they are learning to do better on less land, our increasing numbers will be calling for more land, and thus a coincidence of interests will be produced between those who have lands to spare, and want other necessaries, and those who have such necessaries to spare, and want lands. This commerce, then, will be for the good of both, and those who are friends to both ought to encourage it. You are in the station peculiarly charged with this interchange, and who have it peculiarly in your power to promote among the Indians a sense of the superior value of a little land, well cultivated, over a great deal, unimproved, and to encourage them to make this estimate truly. The wisdom of the animal which amputates and abandons to the hunter the parts for which he is pursued should be theirs, with this difference, that the former sacrifices what is useful, the latter what is not. In truth, the ultimate point

---

[43] Jefferson to George Flower, from Poplar Forest, Sept. 12, 1817, in Lipscomb and Bergh ed., 15:139-142; and Washington ed., 7:83-85. For an account of Flower's colony, see George Flower, *History of the English Settlement in Edwards County, Illinois* (Chicago, 1882).

of rest and happiness for them is to let our settlements and theirs meet and blend together, to intermix, and become one people. . . .[44]

. . . . The aboriginal inhabitants of these countries I have regarded with the commiseration their history inspires. Endowed with the faculties and the rights of men, breathing an ardent love of liberty and independence, and occupying a country which left them no desire but to be undisturbed, the stream of overflowing population from other regions directed itself on these shores; without power to divert or habits to contend against it, they have been overwhelmed by the current or driven before it; now reduced within limits too narrow for the hunter's state, humanity enjoins us to teach them agriculture and the domestic arts; to encourage them to that industry which alone can enable them to maintain their place in existence and to prepare them in time for that state of society which to bodily comforts adds the improvement of the mind and morals. We have therefore liberally furnished them with the implements of husbandry and household use; we have placed among them instructors in the arts of first necessity; and they are covered with the aegis of the law against aggressors from among ourselves. . . .[45]

. . . . The plan of civilizing the Indians is undoubtedly a great improvement on the ancient and totally ineffectual one of beginning with religious missionaries. Our experience has shown that this must be the last step of the process. The following is what has been successful: 1st, to raise cattle, &c., and thereby acquire a knowledge of the value of property; 2d, arithmetic, to calculate that value; 3d, writing, to keep accounts, and here they begin to enclose farms, and the men to labor, the women to spin and weave; 4th, to read "Aesop's Fables" and "Robinson Crusoe" are their first delight. The Creeks and Cherokees are advanced thus far, and the Cherokees are now instituting a regular government. . . .[46]

TRADE PROMOTION

During his years as minister to France, Jefferson sought diligently to promote the trade in agricultural products with Europe. The following report is here included as an illustration of his industry and views on this matter.

The next levee day at Versailles, I meant to bring again under the view of the Count de Vergennes, the whole subject of our commerce with France; but the number of audiences of ambassadors and other ministers, which take place, of course, before mine, and which seldom, indeed, leave me an opportunity of audience at all, prevented me that day. I was only able to ask the Count de Vergennes, as a particular favor, that he would permit me to wait on him some day that week. He did so, and I went to Versailles the Friday following (the 9th of December). M. de Reyneval was with the Count. Our conversation began with the usual topic; that the trade of the United States had not

---

[44] Jefferson to Benjamin Hawkins, from Washington, D. C., Feb. 18, 1803. For the complete letter, see Ford ed., 8:211-216; Lipscomb and Bergh ed., 10:360-365; and Washington ed., 4:465-469.

[45] Jefferson's Second Inaugural Address, Mar. 4, 1805. For the address, see Ford ed., 8:341-348; Lipscomb and Bergh ed., 3:375-383; J. D. Richardson, ed., *A Compilation of the Messages and Papers of the Presidents*, 1:378-382 (Washington, 1896); and Washington ed., 8:40-45.

[46] Jefferson to John Jay, from Monticello, Apr. 7, 1809. For the complete letter, see Lipscomb and Bergh ed., 12:270-271; and Washington ed., 5:440.

yet learned the way to France, but continued to centre in England, though no longer obliged by law to go there. I observed, that the real cause of this was to be found in the difference of the commercial arrangements in the two countries; that merchants would not, and could not trade but where there was to be some gain; that the commerce between two countries could not be kept up, but by an exchange of commodities; that, if an American merchant was forced to carry his produce to London, it could not be expected he would make a voyage from thence to France, with the money, to lay it out here; and, in like manner, that if he could bring his commodities, with advantage, to this country, he would not make another voyage to England, with the money, to lay it out there, but would take in exchange the merchandise of this country. The Count de Vergennes agreed to this, and particularly that where there was no exchange of merchandise, there could be no durable commerce; and that it was natural for merchants to take their returns in the port where they sold their cargo. I desired his permission, then, to take a summary view of the productions of the United States, that we might see which of them could be brought here to advantage.

1. Rice. France gets from the Mediterranean a rice not so good indeed, but cheaper than ours. He said that they bought of our rice, but that they got from Egypt also, rice of a very fine quality. I observed that such was the actual state of their commerce, in that article, that they take little from us. 2. Indigo. They make a plenty in their own colonies. He observed that they did, and that they thought it better than ours. 3. Flour, fish, and provisions of all sorts, they produce for themselves. That these articles might, therefore, be considered as not existing, for commerce, between the United States and the kingdom of France.

I proceeded to those capable of becoming objects of exchange between the two nations. 1. Peltry and furs. Our posts being in the hands of the English, we are cut off from that article. I am not sure even, whether we are not obliged to buy of them, for our own use. When these posts are given up, if ever they are, we shall be able to furnish France with skins and furs, to the amount of two millions of livres, in exchange for her merchandise; but at present, these articles are to be counted as nothing. 2. Potash. An experiment is making whether this can be brought here. We hope it may, but at present it stands for nothing. He observed that it was much wanted in France, and he thought it would succeed. 3. Naval stores. Trials are also making on these, as subjects of commerce with France. They are heavy, and the voyage long. The result, therefore, is doubtful. At present, they are as nothing in our commerce with this country. 4. Whale oil. I told him I had great hopes that the late diminution of duty would enable us to bring this article, with advantage, to France; that a merchant was just arrived (Mr. Barrett) who proposed to settle at L'Orient, for the purpose of selling the cargoes of this article, and choosing the returns. That he had informed me, that in the first year, it would be necessary to take one-third in money, and the remainder only in merchandise; because the fishermen require, indispensably, some money. But he thought that after the first year, the merchandise of the preceding year, would always produce money for the ensuing one, and that the whole amount would continue to be taken annually afterwards, in merchandise. I added, that though the diminution of duty was expressed to be but for one year, yet I hoped they would find their advantage in renewing and continuing it; for that if they intended really to admit it for one year only, the fishermen would not find it worth while to rebuild their vessels, and to prepare themselves for the business. The Count expressed satisfaction on the view of commercial exchange held up by this article. He made no answer as to the continuance of it; and I did not choose to tell him, at that time, that we should claim its continuance under their treaty with the Hanseatic towns, which fixes this duty for them, and our own treaty, which gives us the rights of the most favored nation. 5. Tobacco. I recalled to the memory of the Count de Vergennes, the letter I had written to him on this article; and the object of the present conversation being, how to facilitate the exchange of commerciable articles between the two countries, I pressed that of tobacco, in this point of view; observed that France, at present, paid us two millions of livres for this article; that for such portions of it as were bought in London, they sent the money directly there, and for what they bought in the United States, the money was still remitted to London, by bills of exchange; whereas, if they would permit our merchants to sell this article freely, they would bring it here, and take the returns on the spot, in merchandise, not money. The Count observed, that my proposition contained what was doubtless useful, but that the King received on this article, at present, a revenue of twenty-eight millions, which was so considerable, as to render them fearful of tampering with it; that the collection of this revenue by way of Farm, was of very ancient date, and that it was always hazardous to alter arrangements of long standing, and of such infinite combinations with the fiscal system. I answered, that the simplicity of the mode of collection proposed for this article, withdrew it from all fear of deranging other parts of their system; that I supposed they would confine the importation to some of their principal ports, probably not more than five or six; that a single collector in each of these, was the only new officer requisite; that he could get rich himself on six livres a hogshead, and would receive the whole revenue, and pay it into the treasury, at short hand. M. de Reyneval entered particularly into this part of the conversation, and explained to the Count, more in detail, the advantages and simplicity of it, and concluded by observing to me, that it sometimes happened that useful propositions, though not practicable at one time, might become so at another. I told him that that consideration had induced me to press the matter when I did, because I had understood the renewal of the Farm was then on the carpet, and that it was the precise moment when I supposed that this portion might be detached from the mass of the Farms. I asked Count de Vergennes whether, if the renewal of the Farm was pressing, this article might not be separated, merely in suspense, till government should have time to satisfy themselves on the expediency of renewing it. He said no promises could be made.

In the course of this conversation, he had mentioned the liberty we enjoyed of carrying our fish to the French islands. I repeated to him what I had hinted in my letter, of November the 20th, 1785, that I considered as a prohibition the laying such duties on our fish, and giving such premiums on theirs, as made a difference between their and our fishermen of fifteen livres the quintal, in an article which sold for but fifteen livres. He said it would not have that effect, for two reasons: 1. That their fishermen could not furnish supplies sufficient for their islands, and, of course, the inhabitants must, of necessity, buy our fish. 2. That from the constancy of our fishery, and the short season during which theirs continued, and also from the economy and management of ours, compared with the expense of theirs, we had always been able to sell our fish, in their islands, at twenty-five livres the quintal, while they were obliged to ask thirty-six livres. (I suppose he meant the livre of the French islands.) That thus, the duty and premium had been a necessary operation on their side, to place the sale of their fish on a level with ours, and that without this, theirs could not bear the competition.

I have here brought together the substance of what was said on the preceding subjects, not pretending to give it verbatim, which my memory does not enable me to do.

I have, probably, omitted many things which were spoken, but have mentioned nothing which was not. It was interrupted, at times, with collateral matters. . . .[47]

SLAVERY

In the words of Gilbert Chinard, the biographer, Jefferson "always held that slavery was a national sore and a shameful condition that was to be remedied as soon as conditions would permit. He was looking forward to the time when this could be done without bringing about an economic upheaval; but all hope would have to be abandoned if slavery were industrialized and if slave labor became more productive."[48]

In 1778, Jefferson sponsored the law that prevented the further importation of slaves into Virginia. As a member of the Congress of the Confederation he sought to exclude slavery forever from all the territories in 1784 but was defeated by one vote.

Jefferson deplored the fact that slavery became a political question and particularly that it created a geographical division between the States and thereby threatened the very existence of the Union. In the late years of his life, he was especially stirred by the controversy centering in the admission of Missouri as a slave State.

The following letter from Jefferson to John Holmes, who was active in promoting the Missouri Compromise, explains Jefferson's position on slavery.

I thank you, dear Sir, for the copy you have been so kind as to send me of the letter to your constituents on the Missouri question. It is a perfect justification to them. I had for a long time ceased to read newspapers, or pay any attention to public affairs, confident they were in good hands, and content to be a passenger in our bark to the shore from which I am not distant. But this momentous question, like a fire-bell in the night, awakened and filled me with terror. I considered it at once as the knell of the Union. It is hushed, indeed, for the moment. But this is a reprieve only, not a final sentence. A geographical line, coinciding with a marked principle, moral and political, once conceived and held up to the angry passions of men, will never be obliterated; and every new irritation will mark it deeper and deeper. I can say, with conscious truth, that there is not a man on earth who would sacrifice more than I would to relieve us from this heavy reproach, in any *practical* way. The cession of that kind of property, for so it is misnamed, is a bagatelle which would not cost me a second thought, if, in that way, a general emancipation and *expatriation* could be effected; and, gradually, and with due sacrifices, I think it might be. But as it is, we have the wolf by the ears, and we can neither hold him, nor safely let him go. Justice is in one scale, and self-preservation in the other. Of one thing I am certain, that as the passage of slaves from one State to another, would not make a slave of a single human being who would not be so without it, so their diffusion over a greater surface would make them individually happier, and proportionally facilitate the accomplishment of their emancipation, by dividing the burden on a greater number of coadjutors. An abstinence too, from this act of power, would remove the jealousy excited by the undertaking of Congress to regulate the condition of the different descriptions of men composing a State. This certainly is the exclusive right of every State, which nothing in the Constitution has taken from them and given to the General Government. Could Congress, for example, say, that the non-freemen of Connecticut shall be freemen, or that they shall not emigrate into any other State?

---

[47] Jefferson's "Report of a Conference with the Count de Vergennes on the Subject of the Commerce of the United States with France," Dec. 9, 1785, in Ford ed., 4: 117-122; Lipscomb and Bergh ed., 17: 28-36; and Washington ed., 9: 230-235.

[48] Gilbert Chinard, *Thomas Jefferson; The Apostle of Americanism*, 492 (Boston, 1929).

I regret that I am now to die in the belief, that the useless sacrifice of themselves by the generation of 1776, to acquire self-government and happiness in their country, is to be thrown away by the unwise and unworthy passions of their sons, and that my only consolation is to be, that I live not to weep over it. If they would but dispassionately weigh the blessings they will throw away, against an abstract principle more likely to be effected by union than by scission, they would pause before they would perpetrate this act of suicide on themselves, and of treason against the hopes of the world. To yourself, as the faithful advocate of the Union, I tender the offering of my high esteem and respect.[49]

PATENTS

Shortly after the organization of the present Federal Government, Congress authorized the Secretary of State to issue patents for inventions, and Jefferson is, therefore, often referred to as the Father of the Patent Office.[50] He gave personal consideration to every application for a patent that was filed between 1790 and 1793 and was consulted concerning them long after his resignation as Secretary of State. At the time, many held that the granting of a patent was equivalent to the creation of a monopoly. As Jefferson considered monopolies inimical to popular government, he proceeded with caution in handling patent applications.

However, the following letter to Whitney shows not only Jefferson's caution but his desire to welcome devices that were a labor-saving boon to mankind. The second letter manifests an amazingly detailed knowledge of the history of milling devices and provides a summary of the principles that Jefferson thought should be applied in passing on applications for patents.

The Cotton Gin

Your favor of Oct. 19 enclosing a drawing of your cotton gin was received on the 6th inst. The only requisite of the law now uncomplied with is the forwarding of a model, which being received, your patent may be made out and delivered to you immediately. As the State of Virginia, of which I am, carries on household manufacture of cotton to a great extent, as I also do myself, and one of our great embarrassments is the cleaning the cotton of the seeds, I feel a considerable interest in the success of your invention for family use. Permit me, therefore to ask information from you on these points: Has the machine been thoroughly tried in the ginning of cotton, or, is it yet but a machine of theory? What quantity of cotton has it cleaned on an average of several days, and worked by hand, and by how many hands? What will be the cost of one of them to be worked by hand? Favorable answers to these questions would induce me to engage one of them to be forwarded to Richmond for me.

Wishing to hear from you on the subject, I am, Sir, Your most obed't servant.[51]

Mills and Milling

Your letter of August 3d asking information on the subject of Mr. Oliver Evans' exclusive right to the use of what he calls his Elevators, Conveyers, and Hopper-boys,

---

[49]Jefferson to John Holmes, from Monticello, Apr. 22, 1820, in Ford ed., 10:157-158; Lipscomb and Bergh ed., 15:248-250; and Washington ed., 7:159-160.

[50]See William I. Wyman, "Thomas Jefferson and the Patent System," Patent Office Society, *Journal*, 1:5-8 (1918).

[51]Jefferson to Eli Whitney, from Germantown, Pa., Nov. 16, 1793, in Ford ed., 6:448. For details, see F. L. Lewton, "Historical Notes on the Cotton Gin," Smithsonian Institution, *Annual Report*, 1937, p. 549-563, illus.

has been duly received. My wish to see new inventions encouraged, and old ones brought again into useful notice, has made me regret the circumstances which have followed the expiration of his first patent. I did not expect the retrospection which has been given to the reviving law. For although the second proviso seemed not so clear as it ought to have been, yet it appeared susceptible of a just construction; and the retrospective one being contrary to natural right, it was understood to be a rule of law that where the words of a statute admit of two constructions, the one just and the other unjust, the former is to be given them. The first proviso takes care of those who had lawfully used Evans' improvements under the first patent; the second was meant for those who had lawfully erected and used them after that patent expired, declaring they "should not be liable to damages therefor." These words may indeed be restrained to uses already past, but as there is parity of reason for those to come, there should be parity of law. Every man should be protected in his lawful acts, and be certain that no *ex post facto* law shall punish or endamage him for them. But he is endamaged, if forbidden to use a machine lawfully erected, at considerable expense, unless he will pay a new and unexpected price for it. The proviso says that he who erected and used lawfully should not be liable to pay damages. But if the proviso had been omitted, would not the law, construed by natural equity, have said the same thing. In truth both provisos are useless. And shall useless provisos, inserted *pro majori cautela* only, authorize inferences against justice? The sentiment that *ex post facto* laws are against natural right, is so strong in the United States, that few, if any, of the State constitutions have failed to proscribe them. The federal constitution indeed interdicts them in criminal cases only; but they are equally unjust in civil as in criminal cases, and the omission of a caution which would have been right, does not justify the doing what is wrong. Nor ought it to be presumed that the Legislature meant to use a phrase in an unjustifiable sense, if by rules of construction it can be ever strained to what is just. The law books abound with similar instances of the care the judges take of the public integrity. Laws, moreover, abridging the natural right of the citizen, should be restrained by rigorous constructions within their narrowest limits.

Your letter, however, points to a much broader question, whether what have received from Mr. Evans the new and proper name of Elevators, are of his invention. Because, if they are not, his patent gives him no right to obstruct others in the use of what they possessed before. I assume it is a Lemma, that it is the invention of the machine itself, which is to give a patent right, and not the application of it to any particular purpose, of which it is susceptible. If one person invents a knife convenient for pointing our pens, another cannot have a patent right for the same knife to point our pencils. A compass was invented for navigating the sea; another could not have a patent right for using it to survey land. A machine for threshing *wheat* has been invented in Scotland; a second person cannot get a patent right for the same machine to thresh *oats*, a third *rye*, a fourth *peas*, a fifth *clover*, etc. A string of buckets is invented and used for raising water, ore, etc., can a second have a patent right to the same machine for raising wheat, a third oats, a fourth rye, a fifth peas, etc.? The question then whether such a string of buckets was invented first by Oliver Evans, is a mere question of fact in mathematical history. Now, turning to such books only as I happen to possess, I find abundant proof that this simple machinery has been in use from time immemorial. Doctor Shaw, who visited Egypt and the Barbary coast in the years 1727-8-9, in the margin of his map of Egypt, gives us the figure of what he calls a Persian wheel, which is a string of round cups or buckets hanging on a pulley, over which they revolved, bringing up water from a well and delivering it into a trough above. He found this used at Cairo, in a well 264 feet deep, which the inhabitants believe to have been the work of the patriarch Joseph. Shaw's travels, 341, Oxford edition of 1738 in folio, and the Universal History, I. 416, speaking of the manner of watering the higher lands in Egypt, says, "formerly they made use of Archimedes' screw, thence named the Egyptian pump, but they now generally use wheels (wallowers) which carry a rope or chain of earthen pots holding about seven or eight quarts apiece, and draw the water from the canals. There are besides a vast number of wells in Egypt, from which the water is drawn in the same manner to water the gardens and fruit trees; so that it is no exaggeration to say, that there are in Egypt above 200,000 oxen daily employed in this labor." Shaw's name of Persian wheel has been since given more particularly to a wheel with buckets, either fixed or suspended on pins, at its periphery. Mortimer's husbandry, I. 18, Duhamel III. II., Ferguson's Mechanic's plate, XIII; but his figure, and the verbal description of the Universal History, prove that the string of buckets is meant under that name. His figure differs from Evans' construction in the circumstances of the buckets being round, and strung through their bottom on a chain. But it is the principle, to wit, a string of buckets, which constitutes the invention, not the form of the buckets, round, square, or hexagon; nor the manner of attaching them, nor the material of the connecting band, whether chain, rope, or leather. Vitruvius, L. x. c. 9, describes this machinery as a windlass, on which is a chain descending to the water, with vessels of copper attached to it; the windlass being turned, the chain moving on it will raise the vessel, which in passing over the windlass will empty the water they have brought up into a reservoir. And Perrault, in his edition of Vitruvius, Paris, 1684, folio plates 61, 62, gives us three forms of these water elevators, in one of which the buckets are square, as Mr. Evans' are. Bossuet, Histoire des Mathematiques, i. 86, says, "the drum wheel, the wheel with buckets and the *Chapelets*, are hydraulic machines which come to us from the ancients. But we are ignorant of the time when they began to be put into use." The *Chapelets* are the revolving bands of the buckets which Shaw calls the Persian wheel, the moderns a chain-pump, and Mr. Evans elevators. The next of my books in which I find these elevators is Wolf's Cours de Mathematiques, i. 370, and plate 1, Paris, 1747, 8vo; here are two forms. In one of them the buckets are square, attached to two chains, passing over a cylinder or wallower at top, and under another at bottom, by which they are made to revolve. It is a nearly exact representation of Evans' Elevators. But a more exact one is to be seen in Desagulier's Experimental Philosophy, ii. plate 34; in the Encyclopedie de Diderot et D'Alembert, 8vo edition of Lausanne, first volume of plates in the four subscribed Hydraulique. Norie, is one where round eastern pots are tied by their collars between two endless ropes suspended on a revolving lantern or wallower. This is said to have been used for raising ore out of a mine. In a book which I do not possess, L'Architecture Hidraulique de Belidor, the second volume of which is said [De la Lande's continuation of Montuclas' Histoire de Mathematiques, iii. 711] to contain a detail of all the pumps, ancient and modern, hydraulic machines, fountains, wells, etc., I have no doubt this Persian wheel, chain pump, chapelets, elevators, by whichever name you choose to call it, will be found in various forms. The last book I have to quote for it is Prony's Architecture Hydraulique i., Avertissement vii., and § 648, 649, 650. In the latter of which passages he observes that the first idea which occurs for raising water is to lift it in a bucket by hand. When the water lies too deep to be reached by hand, the bucket is suspended by a chain and let down over a pulley or windlass. If it be desired to raise a continued stream of water, the simplest means which offers itself to the mind is to attach to an endless chain or cord a number of pots or buckets, so disposed that, the chain being suspended on a lanthorn or wallower above, and plunged in water below, the buckets may descend and ascend alternately, filling themselves at bottom and emptying at a certain height above, so as to give a constant stream. Some years before the date of Mr. Evans' patent, a Mr. Martin of Caroline county in this State, constructed a drill-plough, in which he used the band of buckets for elevating the grain from the box into the funnel, which let them down into the furrow. He had bands with different sets of buckets adapted to the size of peas, of turnip seed, etc. I have used this machine for sowing Benni seed also, and propose to have a band of buckets for drilling Indian Corn, and another for wheat. Is it possible that in doing this I shall infringe Mr. Evans' patent? That I can be debarred of any use to which I might have applied my drill, when I bought it, by a patent issued after I bought it?

These verbal descriptions, applying so exactly to Mr. Evans' elevators, and the drawings exhibited to the eye, flash conviction both on reason and the senses that there is nothing new in these elevators but their being strung together on a strap of leather. If this strap of leather be an invention, entitling the inventor to a patent right, it can only extend to the strap, and the use of the string of buckets must remain free to be connected by chains, ropes, a strap of hempen girthing, or any other substance except leather. But, indeed, Mr. Martin had before used the strap of leather.

The screw of Archimedes is as ancient, at least, as the age of that mathematician, who died more than 2,000 years ago. Diodorus Siculus speaks of it, L. i., p. 21, and L. v., p. 217, of Stevens' edition of 1559, folio; and Vitruvius, xii. The cutting of its spiral worm into sections for conveying flour or grain, seems to have been an invention of Mr. Evans, and to be a fair subject of a patent right. But it cannot take away from others the use of Archimedes' screw with its perpetual spiral, for any purposes of which it is susceptible.

The hopper-boy is an useful machine, and so far as I know, original.

It has been pretended by some, (and in England especially,) that inventors have a natural and exclusive right to their inventions, and not merely for their own lives, but inheritable to their heirs. But while it is a moot question whether the origin of any kind of property is derived from nature at all, it would be singular to admit a natural and even an hereditary right to inventors. It is agreed by those who have seriously considered the subject, that no individual has, of natural right, a separate property in an acre of land, for instance. By an universal law, indeed, whatever, whether fixed or movable, belongs to all men equally and in common, is the property for the moment of him who occupies it, but when he relinquishes the occupation, the property goes with it. Stable ownership is the gift of social law, and is given late in the progress of society. It would be curious then, if an idea, the fugitive fermentation of an individual brain, could, of natural right, be claimed in exclusive and stable property. If nature has made any one thing less susceptible than all others of exclusive property, it is the action of the thinking power called an idea, which an individual may exclusively possess as long as he keeps it to himself; but the moment it is divulged, it forces itself into the possession of every one, and the receiver cannot dispossess himself of it. Its peculiar character, too, is that no one possesses the less, because every other possesses the whole of it. He who receives an idea from me, receives instruction himself without lessening mine; as he who lights his taper at mine, receives light without darkening me. That ideas should freely spread from one to another over the globe, for the moral and mutual instruction of man, and improvement of his condition, seems to have been peculiarly and benevolently designed by nature, when she made them, like fire, expansible over all space, without lessening their density in any point, and like the air in which we breathe, move, and have our physical being, incapable of confinement or exclusive appropriation. Inventions then cannot, in nature, be a subject of property. Society may give an exclusive right to the profits arising from them, as an encouragement to men to pursue ideas which may produce utility, but this may or may not be done, according to the will and convenience of the society, without claim or complaint from any body. Accordingly, it is a fact, as far as I am informed, that England was, until we copied her, the only country on earth which ever, by a general law, gave a legal right to the exclusive use of an idea. In some other countries it is sometimes done, in a great case, and by a special and personal act, but, generally speaking, other nations have thought that these monopolies produce more embarrassment than advantage to society; and it may be observed that the nations which refuse monopolies of invention, are as fruitful as England in new and useful devices.

Considering the exclusive right to invention as given not of natural right, but for the benefit of society, I know well the difficulty of drawing a line between the things which are worth to the public the embarrassment of an exclusive patent, and those which are not. As a member of the patent board for several years, while the law authorized a board to grant or refuse patents, I saw with what slow progress a system of general rules could be matured. Some, however, were established by that board. One of these was, that a machine of which we were possessed, might be applied by every man to any use of which it is susceptible, and that this right ought not to be taken from him and given to a monopolist, because the first perhaps had occasion so to apply it. Thus a screw for crushing plaster might be employed for crushing corn-cobs. And a chain-pump for raising water might be used for raising wheat: this being merely a change of application. Another rule was that a ohange of material should not give title to a patent. As the making a ploughshare of cast rather than of wrought iron; a comb of iron instead of horn or of ivory, or the connecting buckets by a band of leather rather than of hemp or iron. A third was that a mere change of form should give no right to a patent, as a high-quartered shoe instead of a low one; a round hat instead of a three-square; or a square bucket instead of a round one. But for this rule, all the changes of fashion in dress would have been under the tax of patentees. These were among the rules which the uniform decisions of the board had already established, and under each of them Mr. Evans' patent would have been refused. First, because it was a mere change of application of the chain-pump, from raising water to raise wheat. Secondly, because the using a leathern instead of a hempen band, was a mere change of material; and thirdly, square buckets instead of round, are only a change of form, and the ancient forms, too, appear to have been indifferently square or round. But there were still abundance of cases which could not be brought under rule, until they should have presented themselves under all their aspects; and these investigations occupying more time of the members of the board than they could spare from higher duties, the whole was turned over to the judiciary, to be matured into a system, under which every one might know when his actions were safe and lawful. Instead of refusing a patent in the first instance, as the board was authorized to do, the patent now issues of course, subject to be declared void on such principles as should be established by the courts of law. This business, however, is but little analogous to their course of reading, since we might in vain turn over all the lubberly volumes of the law to find a single ray which would lighten the path of the mechanic or the mathematician. It is more within the information of a board of academical professors, and a previous refusal of patent would better guard our citizens against harassment by lawsuits. But England had given it to her judges, and the usual predominancy of her examples carried it to ours.

It happened that I had myself a mill built in the interval between Mr. Evans' first and second patents. I was living in Washington, and left the construction to the millwright. I did not even know he had erected elevators, conveyers and hopper-boys, until I learnt it by an application from Mr. Evans' agent for the patent price. Although I had no idea he had a right to it by law, (for no judicial decision had then been given,) yet I did not hesitate to remit to Mr. Evans the old and moderate patent price, which was what he then asked, from a wish to encourage even the useful revival of ancient inventions. But I then expressed my opinion of the law in a letter, either to Mr. Evans or to his agent.

I have thus, Sir, at your request, given you the facts and ideas which occur to me on this subject. I have done it without reserve, although I have not the pleasure of knowing you personally. In thus frankly committing myself to you, I trust you will feel it as a point of honor and candor, to make no use of my letter which might bring disquietude on myself. And particularly, I should be unwilling to be brought into any difference with Mr. Evans, whom, however, I believe too reasonable to take offence at an honest difference of opinion. I esteem him much, and sincerely wish him wealth and honor. I deem him a valuable citizen, of uncommon ingenuity and usefulness. And had I not esteemed still more the establishment of sound principles, I should now have been silent. If any of the matter I have offered can promote that object, I have no objection to its being so used; if it offers nothing new, it will of course not be used at all. I have gone with some minuteness into the mathematical history of the elevator, because it belongs to a branch of science in which, as I have before observed, it is not incumbent on lawyers to be learned; and it is possible, therefore, that some of the proofs I have quoted may have escaped on their former arguments. On the law of the subject I should not have touched, because more familiar to those who have already discussed it; but I wished to state my own view of it merely in justification of myself, my name and approbation being subscribed to the act. With these explanations, accept the assurance of my respect.[52]

PLANT EXPLORATION AND INTRODUCTION

Jefferson believed that "the greatest service which can be rendered any country is to add an useful plant to its culture." He was a pioneer in the work of introducing foreign plants into the United States. Although the following letter gives special attention to upland rice and olives, it also provides his comments on other possibilities.

Having observed that the consumption of rice in this country, and particularly in this capital, was very great, I thought it my duty to inform myself from what markets they draw their supplies, in what proportion from ours, and whether it might not be practicable to increase that proportion. This city being little concerned in foreign commerce, it is difficult to obtain information on particular branches of it in

---

[52] Jefferson to Isaac McPherson, from Monticello, Aug. 13, 1813, in Lipscomb and Bergh ed., 13:326-338; and Washington ed., 6:175-183. For a recent criticism of Jefferson's position with reference to Oliver Evans, see W. V. Morrow, "Joseph's Prudence down to Date; The Story of the Grain Elevator," *Northwestern Miller*, 181:115 (1935).

the detail. I addressed myself to the retailers of rice, and from them received a mixture of truth and error, which I was unable to sift apart in the first moment. Continuing, however, my inquiries, they produced at length this result: that the dealers here were in the habit of selling two qualities of rice, that of Carolina, with which they were supplied chiefly from England, and that of Piedmont; that the Carolina rice was long, slender, white and transparent, answers well when prepared with milk, sugar, &c., but not so well when prepared *au gras;* that that of Piedmont was shorter, thicker, and less white, but that it presented its form better when dressed *au gras,* was better tasted, and, therefore, preferred by good judges for those purposes; that the consumption of rice, in this form, was much the most considerable, but that the superior beauty of the Carolina rice, seducing the eye of those purchasers who are attached to appearances, the demand for it was upon the whole as great as for that of Piedmont. They supposed this difference of quality to proceed from a difference of management; that the Carolina rice was husked with an instrument that broke it more, and that less pains were taken to separate the broken from the unbroken grains, imagining that it was the broken grains which dissolved in oily preparations; that the Carolina rice costs somewhat less than that of Piedmont; but that being obliged to sort the whole grains from the broken, in order to satisfy the taste of their customers, they ask and receive as much for the first quality of Carolina, when sorted, as for the rice of Piedmont; but the second and third qualities, obtained by sorting, are sold much cheaper. The objection to the Carolina rice then, being, that it crumbles in certain forms of preparation, and this supposed to be the effect of a less perfect machine for husking, I flattered myself I should be able to learn what might be the machine of Piedmont, when I should arrive at Marseilles, to which place I was to go in the course of a tour through the seaport towns of this country. At Marseilles, however, they differed as much in account of the machines, as at Paris they had differed about other circumstances. Some said it was husked between mill-stones, others between rubbers of wood in the form of mill-stones, others of cork. They concurred in one fact, however, that the machine might be seen by me, immediately on crossing the Alps. This would be an affair of three weeks. I crossed them and went through the rice country from Vercelli to Pavia, about sixty miles. I found the machine to be absolutely the same with that sed in Carolina, as well as I could recollect a description which Mr. E. Rutledge had given me of it. It is on the plan of a powder mill. In some of them, indeed, they arm each pestle with an iron tooth, consisting of nine spikes hooked together, which I do not remember in the description of Mr. Rutledge. I therefore had a tooth made, which I have the honor of forwarding you with this letter; observing, at the same time, that as many of their machines are without teeth as with them, and of course, that the advantage is not very palpable. It seems to follow, then, that the rice of Lombardy (for though called Piedmont rice, it does not grow in that county but in Lombardy) is of a different species from that of Carolina; different in form, in color and in quality. We know that in Asia they have several distinct species of this grain. Monsieur Poivre, a former Governor of the Isle of France, in travelling through several countries of Asia, observed with particular attention the objects of their agriculture, and he tells us, that in Cochin-China they cultivate six several kinds of rice, which he describes, three of them requiring water, and three growing on highlands. The rice of Carolina is said to have come from Madagascar, and De Poivre tells us, it is the white rice which is cultivated there. This favors the probability of its being of a different species originally, from that of Piedmont; and time, culture and climate may have made it still more different. Under this idea, I thought it would be well to furnish you with some of the Piedmont rice, unhusked, but was told it was contrary to the laws to export it in that form. I took such measures as I could, however, to have a quantity brought out, and lest these should fail, I brought, myself, a few pounds. A part of this I have addressed to you by the way of London; a part comes with this letter; and I shall send another parcel by some other conveyance, to prevent the danger of miscarriage. Any one of them arriving safe, may serve to put in seed, should the society think it an object. This seed too, coming from Vercelli, where the best rice is supposed to grow, is more to be depended on than what may be sent me hereafter. There is a rice from the Levant, which is considered as of a quality still different, and some think it superior to that of Piedmont. The troubles which have existed in that country for several years back, have intercepted it from the European market, so that it is become almost unknown. I procured a bag of it, however, at Marseilles, and another of the best rice of Lombardy, which are on their way to this place, and when arrived, I will forward you a quantity of each, sufficient to enable you to judge of their qualities when prepared for the table. I have also taken measures to have a quantity of it brought from the Levant, unhusked. If I succeed, it shall be forwarded in like manner. I should think it certainly advantageous to cultivate, in Carolina and Georgia, the two qualities demanded at market; because the progress of culture, with us, may soon get beyond the demand for the white rice; and because too, there is often a brisk demand for the one quality, when the market is glutted with the other. I should hope there would be no danger of losing the species of white rice, by a confusion with the other. This would be a real misfortune, as I should not hesitate to pronounce the white, upon the whole, the most precious of the two, for us.

The dry rice of Cochin-China has the reputation of being the whitest to the eye, best flavored to the taste, and most productive. It seems then to unite the good qualities of both the others known to us. Could it supplant them, it would be a great happiness, as it would enable us to get rid of those ponds of stagnant water, so fatal to human health and life. But such is the force of habit, and caprice of taste, that we could not be sure beforehand it would produce this effect. The experiment, however, is worth trying, should it only end in producing a third quality, and increasing the demand. I will endeavor to procure some to be brought from Cochin-China. The event, however, will be uncertain and distant.

I was induced, in the course of my journey through the south of France, to pay very particular attention to the objects of their culture, because the resemblance of their climate to that of the southern parts of the United States, authorizes us to presume we may adopt any of their articles of culture, which we would wish for. We should not wish for their wines, though they are good and abundant. The culture of the vine is not desirable in lands capable of producing anything else. It is a species of gambling, and of desperate gambling too, wherein, whether you make much or nothing, you are equally ruined. The middling crop alone is the saving point, and that the seasons seldom hit. Accordingly, we see much wretchedness among this class of cultivators. Wine, too, is so cheap in these countries, that a laborer with us, employed in the culture of any other article, may exchange it for wine, more and better than he could raise himself. It is a resource for a country, the whole of whose good soil is otherwise employed, and which still has some barren spots, and surplus of population to employ on them. There the vine is good, because it is something in the place of nothing. It may become a resource to us at a still earlier period; when the increase of population shall increase our productions beyond the demand for them, both at home and abroad. Instead of going on to make an useless surplus of them, we may employ our supernumerary hands on the vine. But that period is not yet arrived.

The almond tree is also so precarious, that none can depend for subsistence on its produce, but persons of capital.

The caper, though a more tender plant, is more certain in its produce, because a mound of earth of the size of a cucumber hill, thrown over the plant in the fall, protects it effectually against the cold of winter. When the danger of frost is over in the spring, they uncover it, and begin its culture. There is a great deal of this in the neighborhood of Toulon. The plants are set about eight feet apart, and yield, one year with another, about two pounds of caper each, worth on the spot sixpence sterling per pound. They require little culture, and this may be performed either with the plough or hoe. The principal work is the gathering of the fruit as it forms. Every plant must be picked every other day, from the last of June till the middle of October. But this is the work of women and children. This plant does well in any kind of soil which is dry, or even in walls where there is no soil, and it lasts the life of a man. Toulon would be the proper port to apply for them. I must observe, that the preceding details cannot be relied on with the fullest certainty, because, in the canton where this plant is cultivated, the inhabitants speak no written language, but a medley, which I could understand but very imperfectly.

The fig and mulberry are so well known in America, that nothing need be said of them. Their culture, too, is by women and children, and, therefore, earnestly to be desired in countries where there are slaves. In these, the women and children are often employed in labors disproportioned to their sex and age. By presenting to the master objects of culture, easier and equally beneficial, all temptation to misemploy them would be removed, and the lot of this tender part of our species be much softened. By varying, too, the articles of culture, we multiply the chances for making something, and disarm the seasons in a proportionable degree, of their calamitous effects.

The olive is a tree the least known in America, and yet the most worthy of being known. Of all the gifts of heaven to man, it is next to the most precious, if it be not the most precious. Perhaps it may claim a preference even to bread, because there is such an infinitude of vegetables, which it renders a proper and comfortable nourishment. In passing the Alps at the Col de Tende, where they are mere masses of rock, wherever there happens to be a little soil, there are a number of olive trees, and a village supported by them. Take away these trees, and the same ground in corn would not support a single family. A pound of oil, which can be bought for three or four pence sterling, is equivalent to many pounds of flesh, by the quantity of vegetables it will prepare, and render fit and comfortable food. Without this tree, the country of Provence and territory of Genoa would not support one-half, perhaps not one-third, their present inhabitants. The nature of the soil is of little consequence if it be dry. The trees are planted from fifteen to twenty feet apart, and when tolerably good, will yield fifteen or twenty pounds of oil yearly, one with another. There are trees which yield much more. They begin to render good crops at twenty years old, and last till killed by cold, which happens at some time or other, even in their best positions in France. But they put out again from their roots. In Italy, I am told, they have trees two hundred years old. They afford an easy but constant employment through the year, and require so little nourishment, that if the soil be fit for any other production, it may be cultivated among the olive trees without injuring them. The northern limits of this tree are the mountains of the Cevennes, from about the meridian of Carcassonne to the Rhone, and from thence, the Alps and Apennines as far as Genoa, I know, and how much farther I am not informed. The shelter of these mountains may be considered as equivalent to a degree and a half of latitude, at least, because westward of the commencement of the Cevennes, there are no olive trees in 43½° or even 43° of latitude, whereas, we find them *now* on the Rhone at Pierrelatte, in 44½°, and *formerly* they were at Tains, above the mouth of the Isere, in 45°, sheltered by the near approach of the Cevennes and Alps, which only leave there a passage for the Rhone. Whether such a shelter exists or not in the States of South Carolina and Georgia, I know not. But this we may say, either that it exists or that it is not necessary there, because we know that they produce the orange in open air; and wherever the orange will stand at all, experience shows that the olive will stand well, being a hardier tree. Notwithstanding the great quantities of oil made in France, they have not enough for their own consumption, and, therefore, import from other countries. This is an article, the consumption of which will always keep pace with its production. Raise it, and it begets it own demand. Little is carried to America, because Europe has it not to spare. We, therefore, have not learned the use of it. But cover the southern States with it, and every man will become a consumer of oil, within whose reach it can be brought in point of price. If the memory of those persons is held in great respect in South Carolina who introduced there the culture of rice, a plant which sows life and death with almost equal hand, what obligations would be due to him who should introduce the olive tree, and set the example of its culture! Were the owner of slaves to view it only as the means of bettering their condition, how much would he better that by planting one of those trees for every slave he possessed! Having been myself an eye witness to the blessings which this tree sheds on the poor, I never had my wishes so kindled for the introduction of any article of new culture into our own country. South Carolina and Georgia appear to me to be the States, wherein its success, in favorable positions at least, could not be doubted, and I flattered myself it would come within the views of the society for agriculture to begin the experiments which are to prove its practicability. Carcassonne is the place from which the plants may be most certainly and cheaply obtained. They can be sent from thence by water to Bordeaux, where they may be embarked on vessels bound for Charleston. There is too little intercourse between Charleston and Marseilles to propose this as the port of exportation. I offer my services to the society for the obtaining and forwarding any number of plants which may be desired.

Before I quit the subject of climates, and the plants adapted to them, I will add, as a matter of curiosity, and of some utility too, that my journey through the southern parts of France, and the territory of Genoa, but still more the crossing of the Alps, enabled me to form a scale of the tenderer plants, and to arrange them according to their different powers of resisting cold. In passing the Alps at the Col de Tende, we cross three very high mountains successively. In ascending, we lose these plants, one after another, as we rise, and find them again in the contrary order as we descend on the other side; and this is repeated three times. Their order, proceeding from the tenderest to the hardiest, is as follows: caper, orange, palm, aloe, olive, pomegranate, walnut, fig, almond. But this must be understood of the plant only; for as to the fruit, the order is somewhat different. The caper, for example, is the tenderest plant, yet, being so easily protected, it is among the most certain in its fruit. The almond, the hardiest, loses its fruit the oftenest, on account of its forwardness. The palm, hardier than the caper and orange, never produces perfect fruit here.

I had the honor of sending you, the last year, some seeds of the sulla of Malta, or Spanish St. Foin. Lest they should have miscarried, I now pack with the rice a canister of the same kind of seed, raised by myself. By Colonel Franks, in the month of February last, I sent a parcel of acorns of the cork oak, which I desired him to ask the favor of the Delegates of South Carolina in Congress to forward to you.[53]

EXPERIMENTATION

Jefferson not only did pioneer experimentation on phases of agriculture but also assisted others with their experiments and did much to publicize their findings. The first letter that follows includes a report on the experiment in viticulture undertaken by Philip Mazzei, an Italian physician of considerable ability and education who came to Virginia in 1773. The second relates to the experiments of John Binns of Loudoun County, Virginia, with gypsum. Through Jefferson's efforts the work of Binns received wide attention.

Philip Mazzei and Viticulture

Mr. Segaux called on me this morning to ask a statement of the experiment which was made in Virginia by a Mr. Mazzie, for the raising vines and making wines, and desired I would address it to you. Mr. Mazzie was an Italian, and brought over with him about a dozen laborers of his own country, bound to serve him four or five years. We made up a subscription for him of £2,000 sterling, and he began his experiment on a piece of land adjoining to mine. His intention was, before the time of his people should expire, to import more from Italy. He planted a considerable vineyard, and attended to it with great diligence for three years. The war then came on, the time of his people soon expired, some of them enlisted, others chose to settle on other lands and labor for themselves; some were taken away by the gentlemen of the country for gardeners, so that there did not remain a single one with him, and the interruption of navigation prevented his importing others. In this state of things he was himself employed by the State of Virginia to go to Europe as their agent to do some particular business. He rented his place to General Riedesel, whose horses in one week destroyed the whole labor of three or four years; and thus ended an experiment which, from every appearance, would in a year or two more have established the practicability of that branch of culture in America. This is the sum of the experiment as exactly as I am able to state it from memory, after such an interval of time, and I consign it to you in whose hands I know it will be applied with candor, if it contains anything applicable to the case for which it has been asked. . . .[54]

Binns and Gypsum

It is so long since I have had the pleasure of writing to you, that it would be vain to look back to dates to connect the old and the new. Yet I ought not to pass over my acknowledgments to you for various publications received from time to time, and with great satisfaction and thankfulness. I send you a small one in return, the work of a very unlettered farmer, yet valuable, as it relates plain facts of importance to farmers. You will discover that Mr. Binns is an enthusiast for the use of gypsum. But there are two facts which prove he has a right to be so: 1. He began poor, and has made himself tolerably rich by his farming alone. 2. The county of

---

[53] Jefferson to William Drayton, from Paris, July 30, 1787, in Lipscomb and Bergh ed., 6:193-204; and Washington ed., 2:194-202.

[54] Jefferson to Albert Gallatin, from Philadelphia, Jan. 25, 1793, in Lipscomb and Bergh ed., 9:14-15; and Washington ed., 3:505. See also Richard Cecil Garlick, Jr., *Philip Mazzei, Friend of Jefferson: His Life and Letters* (Baltimore, 1933).

Loudon, in which he lives, had been so exhausted and wasted by bad husbandry, that it began to depopulate, the inhabitants going southwardly in quest of better lands. Binns' success has stopped that emigration. It is now becoming one of the most productive counties of the State of Virginia, and the price given for the lands is multiplied manifold. . . .

I hope your agricultural institution goes on with success. I consider you as the author of all the good it shall do. A better idea has never been carried into practice. Our agricultural society has at length formed itself. Like our American Philosophical Society, it is voluntary, and unconnected with the public, and is precisely an execution of the plan I formerly sketched to you. Some State societies have been formed heretofore; the others will do the same. Each State society names two of its members of Congress to be their members in the Central society, which is of course together during the sessions of Congress. They are to select matter from the proceedings of the State societies, and to publish it; so that their publications may be called *l'esprit des sociétés d'agriculture*, &c. The Central society was formed the last winter only, so that it will be some time before they get under way. Mr. Madison, the Secretary of State, was elected their President.

Recollecting with great satisfaction our friendly intercourse while I was in Europe, I nourish the hope it still preserves a place in your mind; and with my salutations, I pray you to accept assurances of my constant attachment and high respect.[55]

SOCIETIES

Agricultural societies were visualized by Jefferson as the focal points of experimentation with and dissemination of better farming methods, labor-saving implements and machines, new crops, and improved livestock. Because of his eminent agricultural contributions, he received membership in many such societies. He held that they constituted a valuable bond that worked for international good will even in times of war. He was also active in promoting the organization of an agricultural society for his home community, and his outline of its objectives might well be taken as a starting point for similar organizations today.

Centers of Experimentation with New Crops

Your favor of November the 23d came duly to hand. A call to England, soon after its receipt, has prevented my acknowledging it so soon as I should have done. I am very sensible of the honor done me by the South Carolina society for promoting and improving agriculture and other rural concerns, when they were pleased to elect me to be of their body; and I beg leave, through you, Sir, to convey to them my grateful thanks for this favor. They will find in me, indeed, but a very unprofitable servant. At present, particularly, my situation is unfavorable to the desire I feel, of promoting their views. However, I shall certainly avail myself of every occasion which shall occur, of doing so. Perhaps I may render some service, by forwarding to the society such new objects of culture, as may be likely to succeed in the soil and climate of South Carolina. In an infant country, as ours is, these experiments are important. We

---

[55] Jefferson to Sir John Sinclair, from Washington, D. C., June 30, 1803, in Lipscomb and Bergh ed., 10:396-398; and Washington ed., 4:490-492. For details on Binns, see Rodney H. True, "John Binns of Loudoun," *William and Mary College Quarterly Historical Magazine* (ser. 2), 2:20-39 (1922).

are probably far from possessing, as yet, all the articles of culture for which nature has fitted our country. To find out these, will require abundance of unsuccessful experiments. But if, in a multitude of these, we make one useful acquisition, it repays our trouble. Perhaps it is the peculiar duty of associated bodies, to undertake these experiments. Under this sense of the views of the society, and with so little opportunity of being otherwise useful to them, I shall be attentive to procure for them the seeds of such plants, as they will be so good as to point out to me, or as shall occur to myself as worthy their notice. I send at present, by Mr. McQueen, some seeds of a grass, found very useful in the southern parts of Europe, and particularly, and almost solely cultivated in Malta. It is called by the names of Sulla, and Spanish St. Foin, and is the Hedysarum coronarium of Linnaeus. It is usually sown early in autumn. I shall receive a supply of fresher seed, this fall, which I will also do myself the honor of forwarding to you. I expect, in the same season, from the south of France, some acorns of the cork oak, which I propose for your society, as I am persuaded they will succeed with you. I observe it to grow in England, without shelter; not well, indeed, but so as to give hopes that it would do well with you. I shall consider myself as always honored by the commands of the society, whenever they shall find it convenient to make use of me, and beg you to be assured, personally, of the sentiments of respect and esteem with which I have the honor to be, Sir, your most obedient, and most humble servant.[56]

Their Dissemination of New Methods

I have received, through the care of General Armstrong, the medal of gold by which the society of agriculture of Paris have been pleased to mark their approbation of the form of a mould-board which I had proposed; also the four first volumes of their memoirs, and the information that they had honored me with the title of foreign associate to their society. I receive with great thankfulness these testimonies of their favor, and should be happy to merit them by greater services. Attached to agriculture by inclination, as well as by a conviction that it is the most useful of the occupations of man, my course of life has not permitted me to add to its theories the lessons of practice. I fear, therefore, I shall be to them but an unprofitable member, and shall have little to offer of myself worthy their acceptance. Should the labors of others, however, on this side the water, produce anything which may advance the objects of their institution, I shall with great pleasure become the instrument of its communication, and shall, moreover, execute with zeal any orders of the society in this portion of the globe. I pray you to express to them my sensibility for the distinctions they have been pleased to confer on me, and to accept yourself the assurances of my high consideration and respect.[57]

Their International Contacts

A little transaction of mine, as innocent a one as I ever entered into, and where an improper construction was never less expected, is making some noise, I observe, in your city. I beg leave to explain it to you, because I mean to ask your

---

[56] Jefferson to William Drayton, from Paris, May 6, 1786, in Lipscomb and Bergh ed., 5:311-312; and Washington ed., 1:554-555.

[57] Jefferson to Augustin François Silvestre, Secretary of the Agricultural Society of Paris, from Washington, D. C., May 29, 1807, in Lipscomb and Bergh ed., 11:212-213; and Washington ed., 5:83.

agency in it. The last year, the Agricultural Society of Paris, of which I am a member, having had a plough presented to them, which, on trial with a graduated instrument, did equal work with half the force of their best ploughs, they thought it would be a benefit to mankind to communicate it. They accordingly sent one to me, with a view to its being made known here; and they sent one to the Duke of Bedford also, who is one of their members, to be made use of for England, although the two nations were then at war. By the Mentor, now going to France, I have given permission to two individuals in Delaware and New York, to import two parcels of Merino sheep from France, which they have procured there, and to some gentlemen in Boston, to import a very valuable machine which spins cotton, wool, and flax equally. The last spring, the Society informed me they were cultivating the cotton of the Levant and other parts of the Mediterranean, and wished to try also that of our southern States. I immediately got a friend to have two tierces of seed forwarded to me. They were consigned to Messrs. Falls and Brown of Baltimore, and notice of it being given me, I immediately wrote to them to re-ship them to New York, to be sent by the Mentor. Their first object was to make a show of my letter, as something very criminal, and to carry the subject into the newspapers. I had, on a like request, some time ago, (but before the embargo,) from the President of the Board of Agriculture of London, of which I am also a member, to send them some of the genuine May wheat of Virginia, forwarded to them two or three barrels of it. General Washington, in his time, received from the same Society the seed of the perennial succory, which Arthur Young had carried over from France to England, and I have since received from a member of it the seed of the famous turnip of Sweden, now so well known here. I mention these things, to show the nature of the correspondence which is carried on between societies instituted for the benevolent purpose of communicating to all parts of the world whatever useful is discovered in any one of them. These societies are always in peace, however their nations may be at war. Like the republic of letters, they form a great fraternity spreading over the whole earth, and their correspondence is never interrupted by any civilized nation. Vaccination has been a late and remarkable instance of the liberal diffusion of a blessing newly discovered. It is really painful, it is mortifying, to be obliged to note these things, which are known to every one who knows anything, and felt with approbation by every one who has any feeling. But we have a faction, to whose hostile passions the torture even of right into wrong is a delicious gratification. Their malice I have long learned to disregard, their censure to deem praise. But I observe that some republicans are not satisfied (even while we are receiving liberally from others) that this small return should be made. They will think more justly at another day; but, in the meantime, I wish to avoid offence. My prayer to you, therefore, is, that you will be so good, under the enclosed order, as to receive these two tierces of seed from Falls and Brown, and pay them their disbursements for freight, &c., which I will immediately remit you on knowing the amount. Of the seed, when received, be so good as to make manure for your garden. When rotted with a due mixture of stable manure or earth, it is the best in the world. I rely on your friendship to excuse this trouble, it being necessary I should not commit myself again to persons of whose honor, or the want of it, I know nothing.

Accept the assurances of my constant esteem and respect.[58]

---

[58] Jefferson to John Hollins, from Washington, D. C., Feb. 19, 1809, in Lipscomb and Bergh ed., 12:252-254; and Washington ed., 5:427-429.

Jefferson's Scheme for a System of Agricultural Societies

Several persons, farmers and planters of the county of Albemarle, having, during their visits and occasional meetings together, in conversations on the subjects of their agricultural pursuits, received considerable benefits from an intercommunication of their plans and processes in husbandry, they have imagined that these benefits might be usefully extended by enlarging the field of communication so as to embrace the whole dimensions of the State. Were practical and observing husbandmen in each county to form themselves into a society, commit to writing themselves, or state in conversations at their meetings to be written down by others, their practices and observations, their experiences and ideas, selections from these might be made from time to time by every one for his own use, or by the society or a committee of it, for more general purposes. By an interchange of these selections among the societies of the different counties, each might thus become possessed of the useful ideas and processes of the whole; and every one adopt such of them as he should deem suitable to his own situation. Or to abridge the labor of such multiplied correspondences, a central society might be agreed on to which, as a common deposit, all the others should send their communications. The society thus honored by the general confidence, would doubtless feel and fulfil the duty of selecting such papers as should be worthy of entire communication, of extracting and digesting from others whatever might be useful, and of condensing their matter within such compass as might reconcile it to the reading, as well as to the purchase of the great mass of practical men. Many circumstances would recommend, for the central society, that which should be established in the county of the seat of government. The necessary relations of every county with that would afford facilities for all the transmissions which should take place between them. The annual meeting of the legislature at that place, the individuals of which would most frequently be members of their county societies, would give opportunities of informal conferences which might promote a general and useful understanding among all the societies; and presses established there offer conveniences entirely peculiar to that situation.

In a country, of whose interests agriculture forms the basis, wherein the sum of productions is limited by the quantity of the labor it possesses, and not of its lands, a more judicious employment of that labor would be a clear addition of gain to individuals as well as to the nation, now lost to both by a want of skill and information in its direction. Every one must have seen farms otherwise equal, the one producing the double of the other by the superior culture and management of its possessor; and every one must have under his eye numerous examples of persons setting out in life with no other possession than skill in agriculture, and speedily, by its sole exercise, acquire wealth and independence. To promote, therefore, the diffusion of this skill, and thereby to procure, with the same labor now employed, greater means of subsistence and of happiness to our fellow citizens, is the ultimate object of this association; and towards effecting it, we consider the following particulars among those most worthy of the attention of the societies proposed.

1st. And principally the cultivation of our primary staples of wheat, tobacco, and hemp, for market.

2d. All subsidiary articles for the support of the farm, the food, the clothing and the comfort of the household, as Indian corn, rye, oats, barley, buckwheat, millet, the family of peas and beans, the whole family of grasses, turnips, potatoes, Jerusalem artichokes, and other useful roots, cotton and flax, the garden and orchard.

3d. The care and services of useful animals for the saddle or draught, for food or clothing, and the destruction of noxious quadrupeds, fowls, insects, and reptiles.

4th. Rotations of crops, and the circumstances which should govern or vary them, according to the varieties of soil, climate, and markets, of our different counties.

5th. Implements of husbandry and operations with them, among which the plough and all its kindred instruments for dividing the soil, holds the first place, and the threshing machine an important one, the simplification of which is a great desideratum. Successful examples, too, of improvement in the operations of these instruments would be an excitement to correct the slovenly and unproductive practices too generally prevalent.

6th. Farm buildings and conveniences, inclosures, roads, fuel, timber.

7th. Manures, plaster, green-dressings, fallows, and other means of ameliorating the soil.

8th. Calendars of works, showing how a given number of laborers and of draught animals are to be employed every day in the year so as to perform within themselves, and in their due time, according to the usual course of seasons, all the operations of a farm of given size. This being essential to the proportioning the labor to the size of the farm.

9th. A succinct report of the different practices of husbandry in the county, including the bad as well as the good, that those who follow the former may read and see their own condemnation in the same page which offers better examples for their adoption. It is believed that a judicious execution of this article alone, might nearly supersede every other duty of the society, inasmuch as it would present every good practice which has occurred to the mind of any cultivator of the State for imitation, and every bad one for avoidance. And the choicest processes culled from every farm, would compose a course probably near perfection.

10th. The county communications being first digested in their respective societies, a methodical and compact digest and publication of these would be the duty of the central society; and on the judicious performance of this, would in a great degree depend the utility of the institutions, and extent of improvement flowing from them.

11th. That we may not deter from becoming members, those practical and observing husbandmen whose knowledge is the most valuable, and who are mostly to be found in that portion of citizens with whom the observance of economy is necessary, all duties of every kind should be performed gratis; and to defray the expenses of the central publication alone, each member should pay at the first stated meeting of his society in every year, _____ dollars, for which he should be entitled to receive a copy of the publication bound in boards.

12th. The first association of _____ persons in any county notifying themselves as constituted to the central society, should be received as the society of the county making a part of the general establishment here proposed; but every county society should be free to adopt associate members, although residents of other counties, and to receive and avail the institution of communications from persons not members, whether in or out of their county.

We are far from presuming to offer this organization and these principles of constitution as complete, and worthy the implicit adoption of other societies. They are suggested only as propositions for consideration and amendment; and we shall readily accede to any others more likely to effect the purposes we have in view. We know that agricultural societies are already established in some counties; but we are not informed of their particular constitutions. We request these to be admitted into their brotherhood, and to make with them parts of one great whole. We have learned that such a society is formed or forming at the seat of our government. We ask their affiliation, and give them our suffrage for the station of central society. We promise to all our zealous co-operation in promoting the objects of the institution, and to contribute our mite in exchange for the more abundant information we shall receive from others.

For these purposes we now constitute ourselves an agricultural society of the county of Albemarle, and adopt as rules for present observance, the principles before stated.

Our further organization shall be a president, secretary and treasurer, to be chosen at the first stated meeting to be held in every year, by a majority of the members present, provided those present be a majority of the existing members, and to continue in office until another election shall be made.

There shall be four stated meetings in every year, to wit: on the first Mondays in January, April, July and October.

The place of meeting, and rules of the society, shall be established, revoked or altered, and new members admitted, at any of the stated meetings, by a majority of the attending members, if they be a majority of those present, not being less than one-fourth of the whole. And, lest the powers given to the greater quorum of a majority of the whole, should at any time remain unexercised from insufficient attendance, the same may be exercised by a resolution of the lesser quorum of one-fourth, passed at a stated meeting: provided it be confirmed at the next stated meeting, by either a greater or lesser quorum, and in the meantime have no force.

Those who for two whole years shall not have attended any stated meeting shall, *ipso facto*, cease to be members. And to ascertain at all times who are the existing members, the names of those attending every meeting shall be regularly entered in the journals of the society.

The president shall preside at all meetings when present, and when absent, a president *pro tempore* may be appointed for that purpose *by those present*.[59]

---

[59] Jefferson's "Scheme for a System of Agricultural Societies," March 1811, in Ford ed., 7:492; Lipscomb and Bergh ed., 17:404-410; and Washington ed., 9:480-484. For a historical survey of this subject, see Rodney H. True, "The Early Development of Agricultural Societies in the United States," American Historical Association, *Annual Report*, 1920, p. 295-306 (Washington, 1925). For data on the society in Jefferson's home community, see Rodney H. True, "Early Days of the Albemarle Agricultural Society," American Historical Association, *Annual Report*, 1918, 1:243-259 (Washington, 1921), and "Minute Book of the Agricultural Society of Albemarle," *ibid.*, 263-349.

LIBRARIES

Jefferson did much to promote libraries as an important agency of general education as well as scientific research. When the news of the burning of the Capitol by enemy troops in 1814 reached him, he hastened to offer the large and valuable library that he had assembled during the middle years of his life as the nucleus of a new Library of Congress. He had intended that Congress "should have the refusal of it at their own price" at his death, but the disaster prompted the tender of its immediate transfer.[60]

The following letters illustrate his enthusiasm for public circulating libraries and his attention to agricultural libraries.

Circulating Libraries

Your favor of March 19th came to hand but a few days ago, and informs me of the establishment of the Westward mill library society, of its general views and progress. I always hear with pleasure of institutions for the promotion of knowledge among my countrymen. The people of every country are the only safe guardians of their own rights, and are the only instruments which can be used for their destruction and certainly they would never consent to be so used were they not deceived. To avoid this, they should be instructed to a certain degree. I have often thought that nothing would do more extensive good at small expense than the establishment of a small circulating library in every county, to consist of a few well chosen books, to be lent to the people of the country, under such regulations as would secure their safe return in due time. These should be such as would give them a general view of other history, and particular view of that of their own country, a tolerable knowledge of geography, the elements of natural philosophy, of agriculture and mechanics. Should your example lead to this, it will do great good. Having had more favorable opportunities than fall to every man's lot of becoming acquainted with the best books on such subjects as might be selected, I do not know that I can be otherwise useful to your society than by offering them any information respecting these which they might wish. My services in this way are freely at their command, and I beg leave to tender to yourself my salutations and assurances of respect.[61]

Agricultural Libraries

Your favor of Feb. 17 came to hand two days ago. I wish it were more in my power to fulfil the request of furnishing you with a full and complete catalogue for an agricultural library. For this first and most useful of all human arts and sciences, I have had from earliest life the strongest partiality. Yet such have been the circumstances of the times in which I have happened to live that it has never been in my power to indulge it. My reading in that line, therefore, has been necessarily restrained, and for practice, I have had still less leisure and opportunity until age had deprived me of the activity it called for. The catalogue, therefore, now inclosed, is sent rather in proof of my readiness, than of my competence, to serve your society. There is probably no better husbandry known at present than that of England, but that is for the climate and productions of England. Their books lay for us a foundation of good general principles; but we ought, for their application, to look more than we have

---

[60]See Randolph G. Adams, *Three Americanists*, 69-96 (Philadelphia, 1939); and Carl L. Cannon, *American Book Collectors and Collecting from Colonial Times to the Present*, 38-49 (New York, 1941).

[61]Jefferson to John Wyche, from Monticello, May 19, 1809, in Lipscomb and Bergh ed., 12:282-283; and Washington ed., 5:448-449.

done into the practices of countries and climates more homogeneous with our own. I speak as a Southern man. The agriculture of France and Italy is good, and has been better than at this time; the former in the age of De Serres, the latter in the time of Cato, Varro, &c. Lessons useful to us may also be derived from Greece and Asia Minor, in the times of their eminence in science and population.

I wish I could have been more copious in that part of my catalogue: but my acquaintance with their agricultural writings has not enabled me to be so. . . .[62]

Catalogue

Cassianus Bassus. *Geoponika. Geoponicorum sive de re rustica libri xx.* Edited by Jo. Nicolao Niclas. Lipsiae, 1781. 2 vols. 8vo.

Cassianus Bassus. *Geoponika. Agricultural Pursuits.* Translated by Rev. T. Owen. London, 1805-06. 2 vols. 8vo.

Scriptores rei rusticae. *Scriptorum rei rusticae veterum Latinorum.* . . . Edited by Io. Gottlob Schneider. Lipsiae, 1794-97. 4 vols. in 9 pts. 8vo. [Cato, Varro, Columella, Palladius.]

Saboureux de la Bonneterie, Charles, ed. *Traduction d'anciens ouvrages latins relatifs à l'agriculture, et à la médicine vétérinaire; avec des notes.* Paris, 1783. 6 vols. 8vo. [a translation of Cato, Varro, Columella, Palladius.]

Dickson, Adam. *The Husbandry of the Ancients.* Edinburgh, 1788. 2 vols. 8vo.

Trinci, Cosimo. *L'agricoltore sperimentato.* Venezia, 1796. 2 vols. 12mo.

Ronconi, Ignazio. *Dizionario d'agricoltura.* Venezia, 1783. 2 vols. 8vo.

Tupputi, Dominique. *Réflexions succinctes sur l'état de l'agriculture . . . de Naples.* Paris, 1807. 8vo.

Lastri, Marco Antonio. *Corso di agricoltura.* . . . Firenze, 1801-03. 5 vols. in 3. 12mo.

Fabbroni, Adamo. *Istruzioni elementari di agricoltura.* Perugia, 1786. 8vo.

Vettori, Piero. *Trattato della coltivazione degli ulivi.* Firenze, 1762. 8vo.

Serres, Olivier de. *Théâtre d'agriculture.* Paris, 1804. 2 vols. 4to. The late edition with modern learned notes.

Duhamel du Monceau, Henri Louis. *A Practical Treatise of Husbandry.* London, 1759. 4to.

Rozier, François, l'Abbé, ed. *Cours complet d'agriculture théorique, pratique, économique . . . ou dictionnaire universel d'agriculture.* Paris, 1785-1800. 10 vols. 4to. Or the 1797-1805 ed. 12 vols. 4to.

Bidet, Nicolas. *Traité sur la nature et sur la culture de la vigne; revue par Duhamel du Monceau.* Paris, 1759. 2 vols. 12mo.

Maupin. *Nouvelle méthode pour cultiver la vigne.* Paris, 1782. 8vo.

---

[62] Jefferson to George W. Jeffreys, from Monticello, Mar. 3, 1817, in *American Farmer*, 2: 93-94 (1820). The second half of this letter gives essentially the same account of horizontal plowing as that given in the letter to Tristam Dalton on p. 46-47.

The order of listing in Jefferson's "catalogue" has been retained, but the authors' names, the titles of the books, and other elements in the entries have been expanded and standardized with a view to facilitating ready identification in present-day library catalogs. In practically every instance, the size noted by Jefferson is accurate, and it has been possible, therefore, to specify the particular editions that he had in mind.

Jefferson's catalog contains 54 items. The first 40 items were apparently listed geographically (ancient Italy, 5; modern Italy, 6; France, 9; Great Britain, 13; United States, 7). Within each of these groups, the comprehensive works are noted first and then the treatises on specific topics. The 7 items following the first 40 are on gardening (English, 4; American, 3) and the last 7 relate to specific crops (asparagus, 1; figs, 1; orchards, 4; bees, 1).

Chaptal, Jean Antoine Claude, François Rozier, Antoine Augustin Parmentier, and Louis d'Ussieux. *Traités sur la culture de la vigne*. Paris, 1801. 2 vols. 8vo.

Lasteyrie du Saillant, Charles Philibert, comte de. *Du cotonnier et de sa culture*. Paris, 1808. 8vo.

Daubenton, Louis-Jean-Marie. *Advice to Shepherds and Owners of Flocks, on the Care and Management of Sheep*. Translated from the French. Boston, 1810. 8vo.

Lasteyrie du Saillant, Charles Philibert, comte de. *Traité sur les bêtes-à-laine d'Espagne*. Paris, 1799. 8vo.

Home, Francis. *The Principles of Agriculture and Vegetation*. London, 1762. 8vo.

Mills, John. *Natural and Chemical Elements of Agriculture*. London, 1770. 12mo.

Kirwan, Richard. *The Manures most Advantageously Applicable to the Various Sorts of Soils, and the Causes of Their Beneficial Effect in Each Particular Instance*. London, 1808. 12mo.

Hales, Stephen. *Statical Essays*. London, 1738. 2 vols. 8vo.

Tull, Jethro. *Horse-Hoeing Husbandry*. London, 1762. 8vo.

Evelyn, John. *Terra; with Notes by A. Hunter*. York, 1787. Gr. 4to.

Hale, Thomas. *A Complete Body of Husbandry*. London, 1758-59. 4 vols. 8vo.

Home, Henry. *The Gentleman Farmer*. Edinburgh, 1779. 8vo.

Young, Arthur. *Rural Oeconomy*. London, 1773. 8vo.

Young, Arthur. *The Farmer's Guide*. Dublin, 1771. 2 vols. 8vo.

Young, Arthur. *A Course of Experimental Agriculture*. . . . Dublin, 1771. 2 vols. 8vo.

Young, Arthur. *Travels in France*. Dublin, 1793. 2 vols. 8vo. [Young's Annals of Agriculture, and many other works, written merely for money, are scarcely worth buying. Those here named contain whatever of his is worth having.]

Brown, Robert. *A Treatise on Agriculture and Rural Affairs*. Edinburgh, 1811.

Hirzel, Hans Kaspar. *The Rural Socrates*. . . . Hallowell, Maine, 1800. 8vo.

Bordley, J. B. *Essays and Notes on Husbandry and Rural Affairs*. Philadelphia, 1799. 8vo.

Taylor, John. *Arator, or Agricultural Essays*. Georgetown, 1813. 12mo.

Peters, Richard. *Agricultural Enquiries on Plaster of Paris*. Philadelphia, 1797. 8vo.

Livingston, Robert R. *Essay on Sheep*. New York, 1809. 8vo.

Philadelphia Society for Promoting Agriculture. *Memoirs*. vols. 1-2. [now 4] 8vo. Philadelphia, 1808-1811.

New York Society for the Promotion of Agriculture, Arts, and Manufactures. *Transactions*. New York and Albany, 1792-99. 4 parts. 4to. [There are some good works published in the Eastern States, titles unknown.]

Miller, Philip. *The Gardener's Dictionary*. London, 1768. folio.

Miller, Philip. *The Gardener's Kalendar*. London, 1765. 8vo.

Abercrombie, John. *The Gardener's Pocket Dictionary*. London, 1786. 3 vols. 12mo.

Mawe, Thomas. *Everyman His Own Gardener*. London, 1794. 12mo.

McMahon, Bernard. *The American Gardener's Calendar*. Philadelphia, 1806. 8vo.

Gardiner, John, and David Hepburn. *The American Gardener*. Georgetown, 1818. 12mo.

Randolph, John. *A Treatise on Gardening*. Richmond, 1793. 16s.

Fillassier, Jean Jacques. *Culture de la grosse asperge, dite de Hollande*. Amsterdam, 1783. 12mo.

La Brousse. *Traité de la culture du figuier*. Amsterdam, 1724. 12mo.

Langley, Batty. *Pomona; or the Fruit Garden Illustrated.* London, 1729. folio.

Knight, Thomas Andrew. *Treatise on the Culture of the Apple and Pear, and on the Manufacture of Cider and Perry.* London, 1802. 12mo.

Forsyth, William. *On the Culture and Management of Fruit Trees.* Philadelphia, 1802. 8vo.

Evelyn, John. *Sylva, Pomona, and Kalendarium Hortense.* London, 1664. folio.

Rocca, l'Abbé Della. *Traité complet sur les abeilles.* Paris, 1790. 3 vols. 8vo.

EDUCATION

Individual and public enlightenment was a basic essential for the complete fulfillment of the political, economic, and social democracy that Jefferson visualized. Throughout his life, he preached "a crusade against ignorance," with emphasis on general education as the only lasting foundation of freedom and happiness. To achieve this end, he drafted a complete scheme of elementary, secondary, and higher education.[63]

In view of the importance that Jefferson attached to agriculture as the basic industry of the Nation, it was practically axiomatic that he include instruction of agriculture in his educational plans. He hoped for a professorship of agriculture at the University of Virginia which he founded but was thwarted by lack of funds. The following selections from his letters indicate the nature of his ideas on agricultural education and the emphasis that he gave to the need of practical research.

Professorships of Agriculture Needed

I have duly received the volume on the claims of literature, which you did me the favor to send me through Mr. Monroe, and have read with satisfaction the many judicious reflections it contains, on the condition of the respectable class of literary men. The efforts for their relief, made by a society of private citizens, are truly laudable; but they are, as you justly observe, but a palliation of an evil, the cure of which calls for all the wisdom and the means of the nation. The greatest evils of populous society have ever appeared to me to spring from the vicious distribution of its members among the occupations called for. I have no doubt that those nations are essentially right, which leave this to individual choice, as a better guide to an advantageous distribution than any other which could be devised. But when, by a blind concourse, particular occupations are ruinously overcharged, and others left in want of hands, the national authorities can do much towards restoring the equilibrium. On the revival of letters, learning became the universal favorite. And with reason, because there was not enough of it existing to manage the affairs of a nation to the best advantage, nor to advance its individuals to the happiness of which they were susceptible, by improvements in their minds, their morals, their health, and in those conveniences which contribute to the comfort and embellishment of life. All the efforts of the society, therefore, were directed to the increase of learning, and the inducements of respect, ease, and profit were held up for its encouragement. Even the charities of the nation forgot that misery was their object, and spent themselves in founding schools to transfer to science the hardy sons of the plough. To these incitements were added the powerful fascinations of great cities. These circumstances have long since produced an overcharge in the class of competitors for learned occupation, and great distress among the supernumerary candidates; and the more, as their habits of life have disqualified them for reentering into the laborious class. The evil cannot be suddenly,

---

[63]For details, see Roy J. Honeywell, *The Educational Work of Thomas Jefferson* (Cambridge, Mass., 1931).

nor perhaps ever entirely cured: nor should I presume to say by what means it may be cured. Doubtless there are many engines which the nation might bring to bear on this object. Public opinion, and public encouragement are among these. The class principally defective is that of agriculture. It is the first in utility, and ought to be the first in respect. The same artificial means which have been used to produce a competition in learning, may be equally successful in restoring agriculture to its primary dignity in the eyes of men. It is a science of the very first order. It counts among its handmaids the most respectable sciences, such as Chemistry, Natural Philosophy, Mechanics, Mathematics generally, Natural History, Botany. In every College and University, a professorship of agriculture, and the class of its students, might be honored as the first. Young men closing their academical education with this, as the crown of all other sciences, fascinated with its solid charms, and at a time when they are to choose an occupation, instead of crowding the other classes, would return to the farms of their fathers, their own, or those of others, and replenish and invigorate a calling, now languishing under contempt and oppression. The charitable schools, instead of storing their pupils with a lore which the present state of society does not call for, converted into schools of agriculture, might restore them to that branch qualified to enrich and honor themselves, and to increase the productions of the nation instead of consuming them. A gradual abolition of the useless offices, so much accumulated in all governments, might close this drain also from the labors of the field, and lessen the burthens imposed on them. By these, and the better means which will occur to others, the surcharge of the learned, might in time be drawn off to recruit the laboring class of citizens, the sum of industry be increased, and that of misery diminished.

Among the ancients, the redundance of population was sometimes checked by exposing infants. To the moderns, America has offered a more humane resource. Many, who cannot find employment in Europe, accordingly come here. Those who can labor do well, for the most part. Of the learned class of emigrants, a small portion find employments analogous to their talents. But many fail, and return to complete their course of misery in the scenes where it began. Even here we find too strong a current from the country to the towns; and instances beginning to appear of that species of misery, which you are so humanely endeavoring to relieve with you. Although we have in the old countries of Europe the lesson of their experience to warn us, yet I am not satisfied we shall have the firmness and wisdom to profit by it. The general desire of men to live by their heads rather than their hands, and the strong allurements of great cities to those who have any turn for dissipation, threaten to make them here, as in Europe, the sinks of voluntary misery. I perceive, however, that I have suffered my pen to run into a disquisition, when I had taken it up only to thank you for the volume you had been so kind as to send me, and to express my approbation of it. After apologizing, therefore, for having touched on a subject so much more familiar to you, and better understood, I beg leave to assure you of my high consideration and respect.[64]

Chemistry Applied to Domestic Objects

. . . . You know the just esteem which attached itself to Dr. Franklin's science, because he always endeavored to direct it to something useful in private life. The

---

[64] Jefferson to David Williams, from Washington, D. C., Nov. 14, 1803, in Lipscomb and Bergh ed., 10:428-431; and Washington ed., 4:512-515.

chemists have not been attentive enough to this. I have wished to see their science applied to domestic objects, to malting, for instance, brewing, making cider, to fermentation and distillation generally, to the making of bread, butter, cheese, soap, to the incubation of eggs, &c. And I am happy to observe some of these titles in the syllabus of your lecture. I hope you will make the chemistry of these subjects intelligible to our good house-wives. . . .[65]

Agriculture's Place in College Curriculums

The difficulties suggested in your favor of the 28th ult., are those which must occur at the commencement of every undertaking. A full view of the subject however will, I think, solve them. In every meditated enterprise, the means we can employ are to be estimated, and to these must be proportioned our expectations of effect. If, for example, to the cultivation of a given field we can devote but one hundred dollars, we are not to expect the product which $1,000 would extract from it. Applying this principle to the present subject of education, from a revenue of $15,000, and with eight professors, we cannot expect to obtain that grade of instruction to our youth, which 15,000 guineas and thirty or forty instructors would give. Reviewing, then, the branches of science in which we wish our youth to obtain some instruction, we must distribute them into so many groups as we can employ professors, and as equally, too, as practicable. We must take into account also the time which our youths can generally afford to the whole circle of education, and proportion the extent of instruction in each branch to the quota of that time, and of the professor's attention which may fall to its share. In the smallest of our academies, two professors alone can be afforded,- one of languages, another of sciences, or of Philosophy, as he is generally styled. The degree of instruction which can be given in each branch, at these schools, must be very moderate. Yet there are youths whose means can afford no more, and who nevertheless are glad even of that. The most highly endowed of our Seminaries has a revenue of perhaps $25,000 or $30,000. They consequently may subdivide the sciences into twelve or fifteen schools, and give a proportionably more minute degree of instruction in each. It has enabled them, for example, to have five or six professors of Theology. In Europe, some of their literary institutions can afford to employ twenty, thirty, or forty professors. Our legislature, contemplating their means, took their stand at a revenue of $15,000, meant for an establishment of ten professors, but equal in fact to eight only. Accommodating ourselves, therefore, to their views, we had to distribute into eight groups those sciences in which we wished our youth should receive instruction, and to content ourselves with the portion which that number could give. On the professors it would of course devolve to form their lectures on such a scale of extension only, as to give to each of the sciences allotted them its due share of their time.

But another material question is, what is the whole term of time which the students can give to the whole course of instruction? I should say that three years should be allowed to general education, and two, or rather three, to the particular profession for which they are destined. We receive our students at the age of sixteen,

---

[65]Jefferson to Thomas Cooper, from Monticello, July 10, 1812. For the complete letter, see Lipscomb and Bergh ed., 13:176-178; and Washington ed., 6:72-74. Cooper was the first professor selected for the University of Virginia. He was a native of England and the son-in-law of Joseph Priestley. After resigning from the University of Virginia, he became president of South Carolina College.

expected to be previously so far qualified in the languages, ancient and modern, as that one year in our schools shall suffice for their last polish. A student then with us may give his first year here to Languages and Mathematics; his second to Mathematics and Physics; his third to Physics and Chemistry, with the other objects of that school. I particularize this distribution merely for illustration, and not as that which either is, or perhaps ought to be established. This would ascribe one year to Languages, two to Mathematics, two to Physics, and one to Chemistry and its associates. Let us see next how the items of your school may be accommodated to this scale; but by way of illustration only, as before. The allotments to your school are Botany, Zoology, Mineralogy, Chemistry, Geology, and Rural Economy. This last, however, need not be considered as a distinct branch, but as one which may be sufficiently treated by seasonable alliances with the kindred subjects of Chemistry, Botany and Zoology. Suppose then you give twelve dozen lectures a year; say two dozen to Botany and Zoology, two dozen to Mineralogy and Geology, and eight dozen to Chemistry. Or I should think that Mineralogy, Geology and Chemistry might be advantageously blended in the same course. Then your year would be formed into two grand divisions; one-third to Botany and Zoology, and two-thirds to Chemistry and its associates, Mineralogy and Geology. To the last, indeed, I would give the least possible time. To learn, as far as observation has informed us, the ordinary arrangement of the different strata of minerals in the earth, to know from their habitual collocations and proximities, where we find one mineral, whether another, for which we are seeking, may be expected to be in its neighborhood, is useful. But the dreams about the modes of creation, inquiries whether our globe has been formed by the agency of fire or water, how many millions of years it has cost Vulcan or Neptune to produce what the fiat of the Creator would effect by a single act of will, is too idle to be worth a single hour of any man's life. You will say that two-thirds of a year, or any better estimated partition of it, can give but an inadequate knowledge of the whole science of Chemistry. But consider that we do not expect our schools to turn out their alumni already enthroned on the pinnacles of their respective sciences; but only so far advanced in each as to be able to pursue them by themselves, and to become Newtons and La Places by energies and perseverances to be continued through life. I have said that our original plan comprehended ten professors, and we hope to be able ere long to supply the other two. One should relieve the Medical professor from Anatomy and Surgery, and a school for the other would be made up of the surcharges of yours, and that of Physics.

From these views of the subject, dear Sir, your only difficulty appears to be so to proportion the time you can give to the different branches committed to you, as to bring, within the compass of a year, for example, that degree of instruction in each which the year will afford. This may require some experience, and continued efforts at condensation. But, once effected, it will place your mind at ease, and give to our country a result proportioned to the means it furnishes, and which ought to satisfy, and will satisfy, all reasonable men. I am certain it will those to whom the charge and direction of this institution have been particularly confided, and to none assuredly more than to him from whom your doubts have drawn this unauthoritative exposition of the public expectations. And, with this assurance, be pleased to accept that of my sincerely friendly esteem and respect.[66]

---

[66]Jefferson to John P. Emmett, from Monticello, May 2, 1826, in Lipscomb and Bergh ed., 16:168-172; and Washington ed., 7:441-444.

SELECTED REFERENCES CONCERNING JEFFERSON

Adams, James Truslow. *The Living Jefferson.* 403 p. New York and London, Charles Scribner's Sons. 1936.

Beard, Charles A. *Economic Origins of Jeffersonian Democracy.* 474 p. New York, Macmillan Co. 1915.

Betts, Edwin Morris, and Hazlehurst Bolton Perkins. *Thomas Jefferson's Flower Garden at Monticello.* 56 p., illus. Richmond, Va., Dietz Press. 1941.

Bowers, Claude G. *Jefferson and Hamilton: The Struggle for Democracy in America.* 531 p., illus. Boston and New York, Houghton Mifflin Co. 1925.

―――――*Jefferson in Power: The Death Struggle of the Federalists.* 538 p., illus. Boston, Houghton Mifflin Co. 1936.

Bullock, Helen Duprey. The Papers of Thomas Jefferson. *American Archivist,* 4:238-249. 1941.

Chinard, Gilbert. *Thomas Jefferson; The Apostle of Americanism.* 548 p., illus. Boston, Little, Brown & Co. 1929.

Dorfman, Joseph. The Economic Philosophy of Thomas Jefferson. *Political Science Quarterly,* 55:98-121. 1940.

Hirst, Francis W. *Life and Letters of Thomas Jefferson.* 588 p., illus. New York, Macmillan Co. 1926.

Honeywell, Roy J. *The Educational Work of Thomas Jefferson.* 295 p., illus. Cambridge, Harvard University Press. 1931.

Jefferson, Thomas. *The Writings of Thomas Jefferson.* Collected and Edited by Paul Leicester Ford. 10 v. New York and London, G. P. Putnam's Sons. 1892-99.

―――――*The Writings of Thomas Jefferson.* Edited by Andrew A. Lipscomb and Albert Ellery Bergh. 20 v. Washington, D. C., Thomas Jefferson Memorial Association. 1904-1905.

―――――*The Writings of Thomas Jefferson.* Edited by H. A. Washington. 9 v. Washington, D. C., Taylor & Maury. 1853-54.

Kimball, Marie. *Jefferson: The Road to Glory, 1743 to 1776.* 358 p., illus. New York, Coward-McCann. 1943.

Malone, Dumas. Jefferson, Thomas (Apr. 2/13, 1743-July 4, 1826), Statesman, Diplomat, Author, Scientist, Architect, Apostle of Freedom and Enlightenment. *Dictionary of American Biography,* 10:17-35. New York, Charles Scribner's Sons. 1933.

Mayo, Bernard, ed. *Jefferson Himself: The Personal Narrative of a Many-sided American.* 384 p., illus. Boston, Houghton Mifflin Co. 1942.

─────── *Thomas Jefferson and His Unknown Brother Randolph.* 42 p. Charlottesville, Tracy W. McGregor Library, University of Virginia. 1942.

Miller, August C., Jr. Jefferson as an Agriculturist. *Agricultural History,* 16:65-78. 1942.

Oliver, John W. Thomas Jefferson, Scientist. *Scientific Monthly,* 56:460-467. May 1943.

Padover, Saul Kussiel. *Jefferson.* 459 p., illus. New York, Harcourt, Brace & Co. 1942.

─────── , ed. Democracy, by Thomas Jefferson. Selected and Arranged with an Introduction. 291 p. New York, D. Appleton-Century Co. 1939.

Pierson, Hamilton Wilcox. *Jefferson at Monticello: The Private Life of Thomas Jefferson.* 138 p., illus. New York, Charles Scribner. 1862.

Randall, Henry S. *The Life of Thomas Jefferson.* 3 v. New York, Derby & Jackson. 1858.

Randolph, Sarah N. *The Domestic Life of Thomas Jefferson.* Compiled from Family Letters and Reminiscences by His Great-granddaughter. 383 p., illus. Cambridge, Mass., University Press. 1939.

Surface, George Thomas. Thomas Jefferson: A Pioneer Student of American Geography. American Geographical Society, *Bulletin,* 41:743-750. 1909.

Thomas, Elbert Duncan. *Thomas Jefferson, World Citizen.* 280 p. New York, Modern Age Books. 1942.

True, Rodney H. Thomas Jefferson in Relation to Botany. *Scientific Monthly,* 3:345-360. 1916.

─────── Thomas Jefferson's Garden Book. American Philosophical Society, *Proceedings,* 76:939-945. 1936.

Ward, James E. Thomas Jefferson's Contributions to Agriculture. University of Virginia *News Letter* Apr. 15, 1943.

Wilson, M. L. Jefferson, Father of Agricultural Science. U. S. Department of Agriculture, *Extension Service Review* 14:74. May 1943.

Wilstach, Paul. *Jefferson and Monticello.* 258 p., illus. Garden City, N. Y., Doubleday, Page & Co. 1925.

─────── Jefferson's Little Mountain. *National Geographic Magazine,* 55:481-503, illus. 1929.

Wiltse, Charles Maurice. *The Jeffersonian Tradition in American Democracy.* 273 p. Chapel Hill, N. C., University of North Carolina Press. 1935.

INDEX

Adams, John..............5-7, 10, 11, 14
   letters from Jefferson...10, 35, 51-52
Adams, John Quincy.................... 6
Adams, Randolph G., cited............. 78
Agricultural History Society........14-15
Agricultural revolution.............15-16
Agriculture –
   Albemarle County.................32-34
   English......................29, 30, 78
   French...........29-30, 66-71, 74, 79
   importance of..3, 7, 14, 23-28, 40, 78
   Indian...........................56-57
   Loudoun County...................... 72
   Virginian..........30-31, 32-34, 71-72
Agricultural Society of Paris. See
   Société Royale et Centrale
   d'Agriculture.
Albemarle County.............32-34, 48-49
   Agricultural society............21, 77
Almonds...........................69, 70
American Philosophical Society.....14, 17
   18, 19, 21, 38, 44, 72.
Architecture........................2, 7
Artichokes.......................33, 76
Austin, Benjamin, letter from
   Jefferson.......................27-28
Autobiography, Jefferson's, quoted.... 54
Asparagus............................. 33
Bacon, Edmund......................... 18
Barley............................48, 75
Beans.............................39, 76
Bedding............................... 47
Benni seed............................ 64
Binns, John........................71-72
Birkbeck, Morris...................... 56
Books, agricultural...............15, 17
   20, 35, 40, 63, 71, 73, 78-81.
Botany.............2, 14, 17, 22, 82, 84
Bowers, Claude G., quoted............. 9
Breeding circuits..................... 50
Brissot de Warville, Jean Pierre,
   letter from Jefferson..........25-26

Brown, Ralph H., cited................ 24
Bryant, William Cullen, quoted........ 8
Buckwheat.........................46, 75
Burwell, William A., letter from
   Jefferson........................... 46
Butter, price......................... 34
Cannon, Carl L., cited................ 78
Capers............................67, 69
Carrington, Edward, letter from
   Jefferson........................... 12
Cattle.......31, 34, 36-37, 38, 56-57, 76
Chase, Samuel, quoted................. 9
Chemistry..........14, 17, 22, 82-83, 84
Cherries.............................. 33
Chickens, price....................... 34
Chinard, Gilbert, quoted.............. 60
Chronology of Jefferson's life........3-4
Church, Mrs. Angelica, letter from
   Jefferson........................... 35
Cities, dangers of..........23-24, 26, 29
Climate –
   Albemarle County.............33, 48-49
   France.......................30, 68, 70
Cloth.............................45, 52
Clover..20, 30-31, 33, 36, 46, 47, 48, 49
Cochin-China rice.................67, 68
Cocke, John H......................... 21
Commerce –
   Indians............................. 56
   place of..........23-28, 32, 52, 57-60
   United States, with France........57-60
Conservation............15, 20-21, 49, 76
Cooper, Thomas, letter from
   Jefferson........................82-83
Cork oak..........................71, 73
Corn (maize).......................16, 20
   30-31, 33, 36, 38, 46, 47, 49,
   64, 75.
Cotton....................52, 61, 74, 76
Cotton gin............................ 61
Crops.........................47-49, 52-53
   See also specific crops.

	Page		Page
Dalton, Tristam, letter from Jefferson	46-47	Fiorin	53
Dana, Francis, quoted	9	Fish, trade in	59
Declaration of Independence	1, 7, 12	Flax	6, 27, 45, 52, 76
Democracy	1, 11-13, 26, 54, 55	Fleming, George, letter from Jefferson	44-45
Diodati, Comte, letter from Jefferson	36	Flower, George, letter from Jefferson	55-56
Divers, George, letter from Jefferson	52-53	Folding	36-37
Diversification	16, 20, 36, 52, 76	France —	
Dogs	17, 50-51	agriculture	29-30, 66-71, 74, 79
Draft animals	34, 38, 39, 45, 63, 76	climate	30, 68, 70
Drayton, William, letters from Jefferson	66-71, 72-73	commerce	57-60
Drills	2, 7, 15, 18, 47, 48, 64	rice consumption	66-68
Du Pont de Nemours, P. S., letter from Jefferson	11	French colony on Tombigbee	55
Dwight, Theodore, quoted	9	Frontier, influence of	1, 23, 24, 26, 27, 31-32, 75.
Economics. See Political economy.		Fruits. See specific crops.	
Education	1, 26, 78, 81, 83	Fuel, study of, urged	76
agricultural	5, 8, 21, 22, 75-77, 81-84.	Furs, trade	58
		Gallatin, Albert, letter from Jefferson	71
Edwards, Everett E., cited	26	Garden Book	2, 16, 38-39
Eggs, price	34	Gardening	16, 29, 36, 38-39, 52-53, 75-76
Elevators, mill	61-66		
Embargo	6, 8, 10, 25, 28, 32, 52, 74	Garlick, Richard Cecil, Jr.	71
Emmett, John P., letter from Jefferson	83-84	Geese, price	34
Endive	33	Geography	2, 24, 78
England, agriculture	29, 30, 78	Geology, Jefferson's views on	84
English colony, George Flower's	56	German immigration	55
Entail	54	Goode, G. Brown, quoted	24
Entomology	2, 17, 18	Gooseberries	52
Erosion	7, 20-21, 46-47, 49	Grain. See specific crops.	
Europe, contrasted with United States	23, 26, 29, 31-32, 82	Grapes	17, 33, 38-39, 55, 68, 71
		Grasses	53, 73, 76
Evans, Oliver	61-66	See also specific grasses.	
Experimentation —		Gray, L. C., cited	44
Jefferson's	2, 6, 7, 37, 47	Great Britain Board of Agriculture	40, 72, 74.
Other	15, 16, 18, 36-38, 68, 70, 71, 72, 73, 75-76	Grist mills. See Milling.	
		Gullies. See Erosion.	
Farm Book	2, 16, 36-38	Gypsum	20, 36, 37, 71-72
Farm buildings, study of, urged	34, 76	Hall, A. R., cited	46
Farming, views on place of	3, 7, 14-15, 23-24, 29, 35-36, 76.	Hamilton, Alexander	6, 9, 11, 13
		Hamilton, J. G. de Roulhac, cited	52
Farmers General of France	59	Hawkins, Benjamin, letter from Jefferson	56-57
Fences, study of, urged	76		
Fertilizers. See Manuring.		Hemp	6, 21, 45, 52, 75
Figs	33, 69	Hemp brake	2, 18, 44-45

	Page
Hessian fly	18
History, agricultural, importance	14-15
History, books	78
Hogendorp, G.-C. van, letter from Jefferson	25
Hogs, price	34
Hollins, John, letter from Jefferson	73-74
Holmes, John, letter from Jefferson	60-61
Homespun	51-52
Honeywell, Roy J., cited	81
Horses	34, 38, 39, 45
Household manufactures	51-52, 56-57, 61
Illinois country	55
Immigration	55, 82
Implements	2, 18-21, 39-45, 57, 76
Inclosures, study of, urged	76
Indians, policy toward	56-57
Indigo	58
Innes, Henry, letter from Jefferson	50-51
Inventions	2, 7, 15, 18, 19, 20, 21, 29, 39-45, 48, 61-66, 74, 76.
Italy, agriculture	79
Jameson, J. Franklin, cited	54
Jay, John, letters from Jefferson	24-25, 28, 57.
Jefferson, Maria	35
Jefferson, Martha	35
Jefferson, Randolph	17
Jefferson, Thomas, writings quoted—	
Addresses	57
Autobiography	54
Farm Book	36-38
Garden book	38-39
Letters to	
———	48-49
Adams, John	10, 35, 51-52
Austin, Benjamin	27-28
Brissot de Warville, J. P.	25-26
Burwell, William A.	46
Carrington, Edward	12
Church, Mrs. Angelica	35
Cooper, Thomas	82-83
Dalton, Tristam	46-47
Diodati, Comte	36
Divers, George	52-53
Drayton, William	66-71, 72-73

	Page
Jefferson, Thomas, writings quoted	
Letters to—continued	
Du Pont de Nemours, P. S.	11
Emmett, John P.	83-84
Fleming, George	44-45
Flower, George	55-56
Gallatin, Albert	71
Hawkins, Benjamin	56-57
Hogendorp, G.-C. van	25
Holmes, John	60-61
Hollins, John	73-74
Innes, Henry	50-51
Jay, John	24-25, 28, 57
Jeffreys, George W.	78-81
Kercheval, Samuel	12
Lafayette, Marquis de	29-30
Leiper, Thomas	27
Lithgow, J.	26
Madison, James, Rev.	12
Madison, James	26, 39, 47, 49-50
McPherson, Isaac	61-66
Page, John	29
Page, Mann	36
Peale, C. W.	36
Rutledge, Edward	9
Say, J. B.	31-34
Silvestre	73
Sinclair, Sir John	40-44, 71-72
Skipwith, Fulwar	52
Stuart, Archibald	51
Washington, George	30-31, 45-46, 47-48.
Watkins, Henry E.	53
White, John Campbell	53
Whitney, Eli	61
Williams, David	81-82
Wyche, John	78
Notes on Virginia	23-24
Report of a Conference with the Count de Vergennes	57-60
Scheme for a System of Agricultural Societies	75-77
Jeffreys, George W., letter from Jefferson	78-81
Jerusalem-artichokes	33, 76
Johnstone, Paul H., cited	23
Kale	53
Kercheval, Samuel	12
Labor	29, 31, 34, 36, 39, 45, 75, 76

	Page
Lafayette, Marquis de	50
letter from Jefferson	29-30
Land –	
holding	54
importance	23, 24, 26, 27, 31-32, 36, 56-57.
laws	1-2, 54-56, 57
policies	1-2, 55-56
prices	33-34
Languages, interest in	83, 84
Leaders, agricultural, importance	15
Leases	29, 30
Legumes	20, 47-48
See also specific crops.	
Leiper, Thomas, letter from Jefferson	27
Lettuce	33
Levant	68, 74
Lewis and Clark Expedition	4, 16
Lewis, Nicholas	38
Lewton, F. L., cited	61
Libraries –	
agricultural	17, 78-81
circulating	78
Lithgow, J., letter from Jefferson	26
Livestock	31, 34, 36-38, 39, 45, 49-51, 57, 63, 76.
Livingston, Robert	17
Logan, William	37, 38
Lombardy	67-68
Loom	6, 52
Loudoun County, Va	72
Louisiana Purchase	2
Machinery, farm	2, 18-21, 29, 39-45, 47-48, 57, 76.
Madagascar	67
Madison, James, Rev	12
Madison, James	7, 18
letters from Jefferson	26, 39, 47, 49-50
Manager of Monticello	18, 31, 46
Manufactures, place of	6-7, 11, 16, 17, 23-28, 32, 44, 51-52, 56, 57, 61, 74.
Manuring	29, 30, 31, 33, 36-37, 46, 47, 48, 74, 76.
Marle	37
Marshall, John	13

	Page
Mathematics, interest in	14, 17, 82, 84
Mazzei, Philip	38, 71
McMahon, Bernard	52
McPherson, Isaac, letter from Jefferson	61-66
Mechanics	14, 17, 78, 82
Melons, Persian	53
Mercantilism	23, 25
Millet	52, 75
Milling	29, 61-66, 67
Mineralogy	84
Missouri question	60-61
Moldboard	2, 7, 18-20, 39, 40-43, 73, 74
See also Plows.	
Monticello	2, 5, 7, 14, 16, 20, 21, 35, 38.
Morrow, W. V., cited	66
Mulberry	69
Mutton, price	34
Nailery	51
Natural history	2, 14, 22, 82
Natural philosophy	14, 78, 82
Naval stores, trade in	58
Navigation, internal	2, 33
See also Commerce.	
Navy, need of	7, 24
Newspapers, views on	12
Notes on Virginia	23-24, 26, 27
Oats	33, 75
Olives	18, 30, 55, 69-70
Oranges	30
Orchards, study of, urged	76
See also specific crops.	
Ordinance of 1784	1-2
Ordinance of 1785	2
Page, John, letter from Jefferson	29
Page, Mann, letter from Jefferson	35-36
Paleontology	2
Patents	45, 61-66
Peale, Charles Willson, letter from Jefferson	36
Pears	53
Peas	33, 46, 47-48, 49, 64, 76
Pendleton, Edmund	54
Peters, Richard	38
Philadelphia Society for the Promotion of Agriculture	16, 19, 21
Piedmont, Italian	67-68

Plant introduction..................17-18
    66-71, 72-73, 74.
Plastering........................37, 76
Plows..........15, 18-21, 43, 47, 74, 76
    See also Moldboard.
Plowing, contour............7, 20, 46-47
Physics...........................17, 84
Political economy, views........23, 31-32
Pork, price.......................... 34
Potatoes...........31, 37-38, 46, 49, 76
Potash, trade in..................... 58
Prices.........30, 34, 39, 47, 48, 49, 51
Primogeniture........................ 54
Public domain.....................55-56
    See also Land.
Randall, Henry Stephens, cited........ 14
Randolph, Thomas Mann.............20, 21
    33, 35, 37, 46, 48.
References on Jefferson............85-86
Rice......................18, 58, 66-68
Richardson, J. D., cited.............. 57
Roads, study of, urged................ 76
Rogin, Leo, cited.................... 44
Rosinante............................ 35
Rotations..........................7, 15
    20, 31, 33, 36, 45-46, 48-49, 76.
Rural economy, study of.....22, 81-82, 84
Rush, Benjamin....................... 7
Rutledge, Edward..................... 67
    letter from Jefferson............. 9
Rye..................31, 38, 46, 48, 75
Sainfoin..........................70, 73
Saw mills............................ 45
Seed-box. See Drills.
Say, Jean Baptiste, letters from
    Jefferson.....................31-34
Shadwell..................1, 3, 15, 16
Sheep............................6, 18
    31, 34, 36, 37, 49-50, 52, 53,
    74, 76.
Silk................................. 17
Silvestre, letter from Jefferson...... 73
Sinclair, Sir John................19, 53
    letters from Jefferson....40-44, 71-72
Skipwith, Fulwar, letter from
    Jefferson........................ 52
Slavery...................33, 34, 60-61
Small, William....................... 16

Société Royale et Centrale
    D'Agriculture....................73, 74
Societies, agricultural...............7, 15
    17, 21, 72-77.
Soil erosion. See Erosion.
South Carolina........67, 68, 70, 71, 72-73
South Carolina Society for Promoting
    and Improving Agriculture.......18, 70
    72-73.
Spinning 6, 52, 74
Steam engines........................29, 45
Strawberries..................16, 33, 52-53
Stuart, Archibald, letter from
    Jefferson......................... 51
Succory...........................53, 74
Sulla.............................70, 73
Swiss colony on Ohio.................. 55
Taylor, John, of Caroline....17, 20, 36, 37
Threshing machines.........2, 18, 39, 48, 76
Timber, study of, urged..............33, 76
Tobacco...............20, 21, 30-31, 59, 75
Trade. See Commerce.
True, Rodney H., cited.......21, 38, 72, 77
Turkeys, price....................... 34
Turner, Frederick Jackson............. 26
Turnips.........................64, 74, 76
University of Virginia................1, 2
    5, 8, 21, 22, 83-84.
Valencienne.......................... 19
Vergennes, Charles Gravier,
    Count de......................57-60
Vetch.............................48, 49
Vignerons.........................38, 71
Virginia, agriculture...30-31, 32-34, 71-72
Virginia Statute of Religious Freedom... 1
Viticulture......17, 33, 34, 38, 55, 68, 71
Vivisection.......................... 6
Wallace, Henry A..................5, 15
Wars, causes..................24-25, 52
Washington, George.............5, 15, 16
    letters from Jefferson.........30-31
    45-46, 47-48.
Watkins, Henry E., letter from
    Jefferson........................ 53
Weaving..........................51-52
Whale oil, trade in.................. 58
White, John Campbell, letter from
    Jefferson........................ 53

Wheat...............................21, 27
    30-31, 33, 36, 37, 39, 46, 47-48,
    49, 62, 64, 74, 75.
Whitney, Eli, letter from Jefferson... 61
William and Mary, College of........3, 16
Williams, David, letter from
    Jefferson......................81-82
Wilson, M. L......................... 14
Wilstach, Paul, cited................. 6
Wines......................33, 55, 68, 71
Wood Jethro.......................... 19
Woodland, study of, urged..........33, 76
Wyche, John, letter from Jefferson.... 78
Wyman, William I., cited.............. 61
Young, Arthur......15, 17, 30, 37, 38, 74
Zoology,........................17, 22, 84

AGRICULTURAL HISTORY SERIES

The Agricultural History Series is intended as a vehicle for presenting the results of research in agricultural history conducted throughout the Department of Agriculture. Edited in the Bureau of Agricultural Economics, with the aid of a Department advisory committee, the series includes monographs issued at irregular intervals as valuable materials and results of research become available.

No. 1. *Some General Histories of Latin America*, by Wayne D. Rasmussen. 9 p. Ed. 2, April 1942.

No. 2. *Some Landmarks in the History of the Department of Agriculture*, by T. Swann Harding. 94 p. January 1942.

No. 3. *Price Administration, Priorities, and Conservation of Supplies Affecting Agriculture in the United States, in 1917-18*, by Arthur G. Peterson. 16 p. November 1941.

No. 4. *The Hoch-Smith Resolution; A Study of a Congressional Mandate on Transportation*, by E. O. Malott. 117 p. July 1942.

No. 5. *A History of Livestock Raising in the United States, 1607-1860*, by James Westfall Thompson. 182 p. November 1942.

No. 6. *The Government and Wool, 1917-20*, by Thomas J. Mayock. 38 p. August 1943.

No. 7. *Jefferson and Agriculture: A Sourcebook*, compiled and edited by Everett E. Edwards. 92 p. October 1943.

World Food Supply

An Arno Press Collection

Agricultural Production Team. **Report on India's Food Crisis & Steps to Meet It.** 1959

Agricultural Tribunal of Investigation. **Final Report.** Presented to Parliament by Command of His Majesty. 1924

Bennett, M. K. **The World's Food:** A Study of the Interrelations of World Populations, National Diets and Food Potentials. 1954

Bhattacharjee, J. P., editor. **Studies in Indian Agricultural Economics.** 1958

Brown, Lester R. **Increasing World Food Output:** Problems and Prospects. 1965

Brown, Lester R. **Man, Land & Food:** Looking Ahead at World Food Needs. 1963

Christensen, Raymond P. **Efficient Use of Food Resources in the United States.** Revised Edition. 1948

Crookes, William. **The Wheat Problem.** Revised Edition. 1900

Developments in American Farming. 1976

Dodd, George. **The Food of London.** 1856

Economics and Sociology Department, Iowa State College. **Wartime Farm and Food Policy,** Pamphlets 1-11. 1943/44/45

Edwards, Everett E., compiler and editor. **Jefferson and Agriculture:** A Sourcebook. 1943

Famine in India. 1976

Gray, L. C., et al. **Farm Ownership and Tenancy.** 1924

Hardin, Charles M. **Freedom in Agricultural Education.** 1955

High-Yielding Varieties of Grain. 1976

[India] Famine Inquiry Commission. **Report on Bengal.** 1945

Johnson, D. Gale. **Forward Prices for Agriculture.** With a New Introduction. 1947

King, Clyde L., editor. **The World's Food.** 1917

Marston, R[obert] B[right]. **War, Famine and our Food Supply.** 1897

Mosher, Arthur T. **Technical Co-operation in Latin-American Agriculture.** 1957

The Organization of Trade in Food Products: Three Early Food and Agriculture Organization Proposals. 1976

Projections of United States Agricultural Production and Demand. 1976

Rastyannikov, V. G. **Food For Developing Countries in Asia and North Africa:** A Socio-Economic Approach. Translated by George S. Watts. 1969

Reid, Margaret G. **Food For People.** 1943

Schultz, Theodore W., editor. **Food For the World.** 1945

Schultz, Theodore W. **Transforming Traditional Agriculture.** 1964

Three World Surveys by the Food and Agriculture Organization of the United Nations. 1976

U. S. Department of Agriculture, Agricultural Adjustment Administration. **Agricultural Adjustment:** A Report of Administration of the Agricultural Adjustment Act, May 1933 To February 1934. 1934

U. S. Department of Agriculture. **Yearbook of Agriculture, 1939:** Food and Life; Part 1: Human Nutrition. 1939

U. S. Department of Agriculture. **Yearbook of Agriculture, 1940:** Farmers in A Changing World. 1940

[U. S.] House of Representatives, Committee on Agriculture. **Oleomargarine.** 1949

[U. S.] National Resources Board. **Report of the Land Planning Committee. Part II.** 1934